# SILENCE MADE VISIBLE
## HOWARD O'HAGAN AND TAY JOHN

# SILENCE MADE VISIBLE

*Howard O'Hagan
and* Tay John

EDITED BY MARGERY FEE

ECW PRESS

CANADIAN CATALOGUING IN PUBLICATION DATA

Main entry under title:
  Silence made visible : Howard O'Hagan and Tay John

Includes bibliographical references.
ISBN 1-55022-167-1

1. O'Hagan, Howard, 1902–1982   Tay John.
I. Fee, Margery, 1948–.

PS8529.H35T398  1992   C813'.54   C92-095256-9
PR9199.3.0474T398  1992

This book has been published with the assistance of a grant from
the Canadian Federation for the Humanities, using funds provided
by the Social Sciences and Humanities Research Council of Canada.
Additional support has been provided by the Ontario Arts Council
and The Canada Council.

Design and imaging by ECW Type & Art, Oakville, Ontario.
Printed and bound by Hignell Printing Limited, Winnipeg, Manitoba.
Cover photo of Howard O'Hagan courtesy University of Victoria Archives.

Distributed by General Publishing Co. Limited
30 Lesmill Road, Toronto, Ontario M3B 2T6.

Published by ECW PRESS,
1980 Queen Street East, Toronto, Ontario M4L 1J2.

# TABLE OF CONTENTS

# ACKNOWLEDGEMENTS

Any project that has taken this long to complete also inevitably collects a long list of people who deserve thanks, some of whom I have never met. Students, colleagues, and librarians at several universities have, over the past decade, generously helped me with my work on Howard O'Hagan, and I would like to thank them all. Margaret Peterson O'Hagan gave me the pleasure of her conversation and kindly granted me permission to examine her husband's papers and to publish some of his work. Similarly, I thank Jonathan Lovat Dickson for his permission to publish the letter from his father, and Kevin Roberts and Ralph Maud for letting me have a copy of "How It Came About." E.W. Strong generously provided the Berkeley Arts Club material and allowed me to publish it. Chris Petter has been consistently helpful from the beginning, as have the whole staff of the University of Victoria Library's Special Collections. Karl Siegler told me a great deal that was of interest, as did Gary Geddes. The list of those who helped with the bibliography is long, headed by Sarah Harvey and Ella Tanner, and including Ann Barrigar, Peter Clark, Susan Fisher, Carole Gerson, Sara Tulloch, and Carla Wilson of the Victoria *Times-Colonist*. Akira Asai, Pat Martin Bates, Maggie Butcher, Ted Davidson, Colin and Sylvia Graham, Rona Murray, P.K. Page, Nelson Smith, Brian Trehearne, Bruce Whiteman, Rudy Wiebe, and the staff of the CBC Archives all provided clues to the discovery of biographical or bibliographical information, as did many of Howard O'Hagan's friends, correspondents, and fraternity brothers. Colleen Donnelly transcribed Keith Maillard's interview with Howard O'Hagan from tapes, and Sherril Barr, Karen Donnelly, and Kathy Goodfriend typed and retyped the text. Part of the work was supported by a grant from the University of Victoria Library, and the department of English at the University of Victoria provided me with the assistance of a work-study student. Finally, I would like to thank my family for their support of this project, especially Gunter and Hugo, who accompanied me on my pilgrimage to Tête Jaune Cache.

# Introduction

MARGERY FEE

When Howard O'Hagan's *Tay John* was reprinted in Canada in 1974, it seemed as if it had appeared out of nowhere. Little was known about O'Hagan, who had produced a brilliant novel clearly based on an intimate knowledge of the country, though it was a novel that was oddly out of step with the developing Canadian canon. Although it was first published in 1939, as was Frederick Philip Grove's realist-naturalist *Two Generations*, *Tay John* has little in common with this or the other novels published that year. In fact, *Tay John* has more in common with Robert Kroetsch's postmodern *Gone Indian* (1973), which was published over three decades later. This collection begins to explain *Tay John*'s distinctiveness by setting it into the context of O'Hagan's life, his early writing, and his reception by readers in Great Britain, the United States, and Canada.

Although O'Hagan's writing certainly deserves far more attention and analysis than it has received so far, the critics who are beginning to work on it have had difficulty acquiring factual information about the author's life and widely scattered publications. I began writing a paper on *Tay John* in 1982 while teaching at the University of Victoria. Much to my delight, I discovered that the university holds several boxes of O'Hagan's papers, including manuscripts and a wide correspondence. That discovery became the first, tentative step toward the creation of this collection. In 1985, the university archivist, Chris Petter, and I wrote to all O'Hagan's correspondents whose letters were in the archives, hoping to discover more about his past. Sadly, many had died; others had encountered O'Hagan only briefly, or related events tangential to our concern with his writing. The recollections in the letter from Lovat Dickson date back the farthest, and I hope they can stand for the many helpful responses we received, all now held in the University of

Victoria Archives. Later, Peter Clark interviewed several of the O'Hagans' friends in Victoria. The unforgettable conversations I had with Margaret Peterson O'Hagan — whose narrative style is at least as fascinating as her husband's — also helped to fill in many of the remaining blank spaces.

The chronology, the result of these interviews and of information gleaned from the letters and papers, makes it easier to understand why O'Hagan seemed to appear out of nowhere. He spent over 30 years living in Buenos Aires, New York, Berkeley, and Sicily. His difference from his Canadian literary contemporaries is in part explained by his sheer physical distance from them, as well as by his involvement with the new fields of discourse, alien to such contemporaries, that were associated with public relations, the international press, and Hollywood, not to mention the California intellectual scene.

Keith Maillard interviewed Howard O'Hagan in July 1979, near the end of O'Hagan's life. Perhaps this interview might more logically have been placed at the end of the collection, but it touches briefly on so many matters that are examined in more detail (one might even say at more pedantic length) in other parts of the collection, that I have positioned it near the beginning. There it serves as a kind of introduction in itself, sparking curiosity, hinting at mysteries, pointing to ideas that might have been pursued further, but that somehow got lost in the turns of the conversation. It also gives us an idea, if only a ghostly one, of what O'Hagan cared about, what he wanted to talk about, and what he wanted to remember.

The writings by O'Hagan included in this collection illuminate some parts of his early life, reveal something of his style (early and late, conventional and avant-garde), and demonstrate thematic and stylistic features that recur in *Tay John*. The tramp steamer *Argus* of "How It Came About" travels the route O'Hagan himself took when he went to Australia after finishing university; "Slim from the Chilcotin" covers more of the same territory; "Accepted by the Penguins" deals with the period in O'Hagan's life when he worked in Argentina as the director of public relations for a British-owned railway. "How It Came About," according to O'Hagan, was his first published story (for O'Hagan's account of writing the story, see Geddes 86); "Slim from the Chilcotin" was published as "The Man Who Took Chilcotin to Australia" in a slightly different form in the Victoria *Colonist* in 1963; "Accepted by the Penguins" does not seem to have ever been published.

"How It Came About" shows the influence of Joseph Conrad in its setting, plot, and character: the sea, the moral lapse followed by violence, and the exotic, inscrutable Ah Lee. Freighted with words that echo Conrad, such as "implacable," "interminable," "unalterable," "immemorial," "impenetrable," and "destiny," the story shows the young O'Hagan imitating what later he would parody. The sonorous, omniscient voice that begins the story is like the voice that begins *Tay John*, but the story lacks the historical and geographical detail unique to the Rocky Mountain region that marks *Tay John* as a New World parody of Old World pretensions to the universal. The sensitivity to racial and social exclusion that drives the story are found in all of O'Hagan's writings. Perhaps O'Hagan's interest in these issues can be traced to his childhood. He grew up in comfortable homes in various small Alberta communities that were composed of people from all classes and nations, most of whom would eventually have come into contact with O'Hagan's father, the local doctor. But whatever the cause, O'Hagan thought a lot more about race, place, and class than was typical of a person of his time.

Significantly, in the interview with Keith Maillard, O'Hagan singles out Margaret Laurence's story "The Loons" for special praise. It is about a doctor's child who tries to make friends with a Métis girl in a small community, where almost all classes and ethnic groups are represented, but each by so few individuals that the ignorance and distance that usually marks social boundaries is breached, with unsettling effects.

One might find just such a set of social conditions on a ship. In "Accepted by the Penguins," O'Hagan does use a ship as the setting for a study that focuses again on social and ethnic exclusion. This autobiographical piece positions O'Hagan, obtrusively Canadian, obtrusively young, on a passenger ship off South America trying to surmount these disabilities. But he is ignored, excluded, and made to feel even more disabled. Ormsby, the other odd man out, finally explains by pointing out that the other passengers, most of whom are British, think they are both South American. Interestingly, once the penguins (doomed, as usual, to symbolize a hierarchical and formal human society) accept O'Hagan, he is gradually allowed into the ship's social circle. He is also able, once more, to see his beloved mountains as he travels overland back to Argentina, where he was working for a British-owned railroad. Society is important to O'Hagan for its power to make him feel accepted and at home, but nature is more important to him because it can do this to an even greater degree.

"Slim from the Chilcotin," another autobiographical piece, begins, as does "How It Came About," on a ship bound for Australia. O'Hagan is thrown together with Slim, another outsider. What suits the Cariboo does not suit Sydney, Australia, but Slim, like Ormsby, refuses to conform, and similarly suffers for it. The mysterious attachment, even loyalty, O'Hagan feels to Slim resembles the odd compulsion Jackie Denham has to understand Tay John. Just as Denham supports Tay John against the forces that would submit him to convention, O'Hagan embroils himself in a fight because of Slim. O'Hagan emphasizes how Australia constructs them both as outsiders: their Canadian experience with horses will not get them jobs on any sheep station. They are seen as defective by virtue of their origins. His last sight of Slim is reminiscent of Jackie Denham's second-to-last glimpse of Tay John: in each case, the two men are separated by a press of struggling humanity, unable to help or be heard by the other. Both Slim and Tay John represent the place O'Hagan himself identified with most strongly: the interior of British Columbia, its horses, its men, its railways, its eccentric and lonely characters, and, above all, its mountains, filled with mystery.

The "Berkeley Chronicles" are somewhat anomalous in the group of writings by O'Hagan included in this collection, as they were not written for publication, but for a small audience of intellectuals, the members of the Berkeley Arts Club, which O'Hagan joined in 1938. These chronicles — written between 1942 and 1947 and now held with the Berkeley Arts Club Papers by the University of California at Berkeley — make it clear that O'Hagan's time in Berkeley may in part account for the avant-garde features of *Tay John*. The flat characters with semisymbolic names, the grotesque and inexplicable events, and the narrative perspective occasionally warped by the narrator's drunkenness, all recur in the novel, even though the setting of the chronicles is the men's faculty club at Berkeley and its civilized environs rather than a mountain wilderness. And the fact that O'Hagan presented some of his stories to the Arts Club for discussion may well have influenced his style. E.W. Strong's memoir and commentary sets these chronicles into a context without which it would be nearly incomprehensible, and it also sheds light on the period when O'Hagan was working on *Tay John*.

Like other writers of the time who had to support themselves by the pen, O'Hagan recycled material. Or, to put it another way, he returned almost compulsively to a small set of themes and characters. W.J. Keith's "Howard O'Hagan, *Tay John*, and the Growth of Story" makes an exemplary start on the task of examining how O'Hagan reworked material over time for a variety of publications. O'Hagan revised many pieces, and a great deal of editorial work is needed before all the implications of these revisions are clear. As "A Note on the Publishing History of Howard O'Hagan's *Tay John*" shows, the revisions between the first and the second editions of *Tay John*, though minor (constrained as they were by the impracticality of resetting more than a few lines), reveal the importance O'Hagan attached to getting the nuances right.

O'Hagan took similar care with the history of the place and time he evokes in *Tay John*. Although he somewhat rebelliously mixes allusions to the high culture of the Western literary canon with those to the low culture of the Canadian West, it only becomes clear that O'Hagan was actually resisting high culture when one examines his regional material. He was careful to get names and cultural details straight. Ralph Maud's "Ethnographic Notes on Howard O'Hagan's *Tay John*" outlines the lengths to which O'Hagan went to do his region and its people justice. His choice of a Métis hero was based not so much on a romantic concept of the exotic other as on his own personal experience of discrimination, which came in part from having been treated like a servant by the tourists he guided, and in part from watching the Métis and Native people with whom he worked suffer at the hands of a bigoted society. It may also have come from his own reception at McGill University, where he was regarded by many (as letters in the University of Victoria Archives reveal) as a bit of a wild man. This is a reputation he may well have cultivated, as he later cultivated the persona of the mountain man, the "old horse handler" (O'Hagan, "Talking" 45).

Ronald Granofsky's "The Country of Illusion: Vision, Change, and Misogyny in Howard O'Hagan's *Tay John*" examines the interplay between vision and blindness, the horizontal and the vertical, change and stasis, substance and shadow, male and female. In his thoughtful unravelling of these dualities, Granofsky tackles *Tay John*'s misogyny, particularly striking when one considers the remarkable insight into women shown in O'Hagan's later novel *The School-Marm Tree* (1977). Of course, that a novel published by a man in 1939 shows traces of misogyny is hardly unusual, as Granofsky's references to several American writers of that time make clear. What is of interest, however, is how O'Hagan's misogyny was deployed in its particular context, and how it changed over time. O'Hagan's comments on women in the interview with Maillard cast some interesting light on the issue, and they also draw connections between *The School-Marm Tree* and the realist romances of Louis Hémon and Martha Ostenso.

As I show in "The Canonization of Two Underground Classics: Howard O'Hagan's *Tay John* and Malcolm Lowry's *Under the Volcano*," the positive reception of a literary work depends on more than its literary quality. O'Hagan's absence from Canada, and his flouting of the realist conventions dominant there at the time he began to publish, meant that he could not be received with understanding in his own country until its literary canon had been opened up by the explosion of writing that took place in the 1960s. Lowry, because he had a clear-cut appeal for an international audience interested in avant-garde fiction, was virtually guaranteed a positive reception for his novel. However, the Canadian literary institution, based mainly in Ontario and English-speaking Montreal, wanted evidence of a national literature, not a novel such as *Tay John*, set on the margins and written in a style that swerved unnervingly between the sophisticated and the grotesque. Reception studies such as this one on O'Hagan and Lowry are particularly interesting when conducted in Canada, where, because the literary market is so small, the number of works that make it either onto the best-seller lists or into the canon is necessarily limited.

The annotated bibliography that concludes this collection, the result of Richard Arnold's determined sleuthing at major libraries in Canada and the United States, not only gives practical assistance, but also makes it easier to understand some of the peculiar mixing of generic conventions in O'Hagan's writing. Highly educated, familiar with writers such as Joseph Conrad, T.S. Eliot, William Faulkner, E.M. Forster, Ernest Hemingway, and Virginia Woolf, O'Hagan wrote for little magazines. He also, however, wrote for newspapers and men's adventure magazines such as *True* and *Argosy*. For some, this would have been like enduring purgatory, but the odd combination of myth, modernism, and pulp press seemed to suit O'Hagan, and his confident handling of this mix accounts for much of *Tay John*'s power as a work of art. Its New World flavour is lacking in nostalgia for the pure, the cultivated, and the European (a nostalgia unlikely to appeal to the audience of American adventure magazines).

In his afterword to the 1989 New Canadian Library edition of O'Hagan's novel, Michael Ondaatje claims for *Tay John* a place in the first stage of the development of the contemporary novel in Canada, grouping it with Elizabeth Smart's *By Grand Central Station I Sat Down and Wept* (1945), Ethel Wilson's *Swamp Angel* (1954), and Sheila Watson's *The Double Hook* (1959). George Bowering links *Tay John* with Watson's novel and with Leonard Cohen's *Beautiful Losers* (1966), commenting that "the margin is the most fruitful place for post-modernism" (131). As Ondaatje notes, this grouping forms an "uncomfortable tradition" of "books that burn and splash on the periphery" (271–72). These works are united by their preparedness to resist the dominance of realist conventions in a variety of ways, for example, through the use of lyricism, parody, myth, and humour (or all of these). In this tradition might well be placed other buried works that are *Tay John*'s near contemporaries, such as P.K. Page's novella "The Sun and the Moon" (1944) (see Atwood, "Canadian" 106–07; Carrington 65). Furthermore, writers such as Ondaatje who have cited O'Hagan as an influence might well be examined as part of this countertradition. Robert Harlow, for example, uses O'Hagan's story "The Black Ghost" extensively in his best-known novel, *Scann* (1972). In an interview with Joyce Carol Oates, Margaret Atwood states that she regards *Tay John* as "cognate" with her novel *Surfacing*, which was published in the same year as Harlow's novel. According to Atwood, *Tay John* resembles *Surfacing* in its refusal to accept a vision of nature as something "wild, untamed, feminine, dangerous and mysterious" that a hero must "struggle with, confront, conquer and overcome" ("Dancing" 76). Perhaps the integration of these peripheral and formally innovative fictions into our concept of the Canadian novel, commonly seen as realist and formally imitative, will permit a reformulation of the concepts of regional and national in Canadian literary criticism.

Recently, theorists of this uncomfortable tradition (one of the things that led Ondaatje to label it "uncomfortable" is that the critics and theorists who promote it are themselves uncomfortable with the very idea of tradition) have begun to integrate O'Hagan into their commentary. For example, Stephen Scobie's *Signature, Event, Cantext* (1989), a Derridean reading of Canadian literature, draws *Tay John* into a wider discussion of the importance of names, and Robert Kroetsch's "The Veil of Knowing" (in *The Lovely Treachery of Words* [1989]) uses *Tay John* as a paradigmatic example of what distinguishes Canadian literature from American. Slowly, O'Hagan is being woven into a discourse from which he was excluded for too long.

Atwood, Margaret. "Canadian Monsters." *The Canadian Imagination: Dimensions of a Literary Culture*. Ed. David Staines. Cambridge: Harvard UP, 1977: 97–122.

——. "Dancing on the Edge of the Precipice." With Joyce Carol Oates. *Margaret Atwood: Conversations*. Ed. Earl G. Ingersoll. Ontario Review Press Critical Series. Willowdale, ON: Firefly, 1990. 74–85.

Bowering, George. "Language Women: Post-Anecdotal Writing in Canada." *Sagetrieb* 7.1 (1988): 131–41.

Carrington, Ildikó de Papp. "Margaret Atwood." *Canadian Writers and Their Works*. Fiction Series. Ed. Robert Lecker, Jack David, and Ellen Quigley. Vol. 9. Toronto: ECW, 1987: 25–116. 10 vols. to date. 1983– .

Geddes, Gary. "The Writer That CanLit Forgot." *Saturday Night* Nov. 1977: 84–92.

O'Hagan, Howard. "Talking to Howard O'Hagan." With Kevin Roberts. *Event* 5 (1976): 41–48.

Ondaatje, Michael. Afterword. *Tay John*. By Howard O'Hagan. New Canadian Library 105. 1960. Toronto: McClelland, 1989. 265–72.

# Howard O'Hagan (1902–82): A Chronology

PETER JAMES CLARK AND MARGERY FEE

1900    Howard O'Hagan's parents move to the Crowsnest Pass region of Alberta, where O'Hagan's father, Thomas F. O'Hagan (born in 1877, in Port Huron, Michigan), MD (Queen's University, 1900), opens a practice that serves patients in Lille, Frank, Blairmore, and Coleman.

1902    Howard O'Hagan is born in Lethbridge, Alberta.

1903    The family lives near Frank, and are there when the Frank landslide takes place.

1909    With his mother, Mary McNabb O'Hagan, and sister Elizabeth, O'Hagan visits his maternal uncle, Donald McNabb, a mining consultant for Republic Steel, in Mexico.

1910    Thomas O'Hagan moves his practice to Calgary.

1915    O'Hagan moves with his mother and sister to Vancouver when his father enlists in the army.

1918–19    Thomas O'Hagan returns from war, having been promoted to the rank of major and awarded the Military Cross. He goes to work in a veterans' hospital on Vancouver Island. Howard O'Hagan attends his first year of university at the University of British Columbia.

1919    He transfers to McGill University, Montreal, for his second year; studies with Stephen Leacock, among others; and joins the fraternity Theta Delta Chi.

1920    O'Hagan's parents move to Lucerne, British Columbia, a Canadian Pacific Railway freight divisional point; in the summer, he works as an axeman for a survey party.

15

| 1920–21 | O'Hagan completes his third year at McGill University. |
|---|---|
| 1921–22 | He becomes associate editor of the *McGill Daily* and receives a BA Honours degree in economics and political science. |
| 1922–23 | O'Hagan enters McGill Law School. In the summer of 1923, he works as a guard for the CPR, escorting a trainload of Chinese indentured labourers who are travelling across Canada on their way from the West Indies to their ship in Vancouver. He then works for Fred Brewster, a well-known guide and outfitter, taking tourists and hunters through the mountains. |
| 1923–24 | He completes his second year of law at McGill, and becomes editor in chief of the *McGill Daily* and sports reporter for the *Montreal Star*. |
| 1924 | The O'Hagan family moves to Jasper when the CPR moves its townsite there from Lucerne. O'Hagan takes one trip for Brewster, and then goes to England as a publicity agent for the CPR, informing prospective immigrants of the advantages of moving to western Canada; this is a job Stephen Leacock helps him to get. |
| 1924–25 | O'Hagan becomes vice-president of the Student Council, president of the Literary and Debating Society, and president of the *McGill Daily*. He graduates with a Bachelor of Law degree, and finds work as a reporter for the *Montreal Star* and the *Edmonton Journal*. |
| 1927 | He travels to Australia, then returns to New York, where he meets Harvey Fergusson, a writer. He lives with a fraternity brother, Arthur William Wallace (Willie), who will become a well-known architect in Canada. |
| 1929–30 | O'Hagan becomes an assistant United States press representative for the Canadian National Railway in New York City. |
| 1930 | O'Hagan works as a publicity agent for the CPR in Jasper. |
| 1931 | In November, he travels to London to sign a contract to work for a British-owned railway in Argentina. He returns to Jasper, and spends the winter skiing in the Tonquin Valley with Fred Brewster. O'Hagan arrives in Argentina with a three-year contract as head of Ferrocaril Central Argentino's publicity department. He may have written |

"The Blue Distance" (an unpublished novel set in New York City) at this time.

1934     He returns to Jasper, but moves to Berkeley on the advice of Harvey Fergusson, who has moved there himself from New York, and is writing novels and film scripts. He meets Margaret Peterson (MFA Berkeley), who has been a professor of fine art since 1932 at the University of California at Berkeley.

1935–39     O'Hagan and Margaret Peterson marry in 1935. The couple spends summers writing and painting on Bowen Island, British Columbia; they also travel to Guatemala and Mexico.

1938     Listed as reporter and short-story writer, O'Hagan becomes the twenty-fourth member (and one of three non-faculty members) of the all-male Berkeley Arts Club.

1939     *Tay John* is published in London by Laidlaw and Laidlaw.

1941     O'Hagan severely injures his leg while working as a stevedore.

1950–52     Margaret O'Hagan resigns from Berkeley after refusing to take an oath of loyalty; the O'Hagans live in Mexico, New York, Guatemala, and San Francisco.

1952     O'Hagan works on a survey crew laying out the underground powerhouse at Kemano, part of the Alcan project at the head of the Gardner Canal in northern British Columbia.

1953–56     The O'Hagans live about five miles from Duncan, British Columbia, at Green Point (near the mouth of the Cowichan River). O'Hagan meets Robert Weaver, producer of the CBC radio program *Anthology*, and novelist Robert Harlow.

1957     The O'Hagans move to Victoria. Thomas O'Hagan dies. While the O'Hagans live in Victoria, between 1957 and 1963, their circle of friends includes many local artists and writers: Rona Murray, Colin Graham (a former student of Margaret O'Hagan's who will become curator of the Art Galley of Victoria), Pat Martin Bates, Elza Mayhew, and Robin Skelton.

1958     *Wilderness Men* is published in New York by Doubleday.

1959     O'Hagan is awarded the President's Medal by the University of Western Ontario for the best Canadian short story published in 1958: "Trees Are Lonely Company." He becomes involved in trying to save the Victoria Market.

1960    *Tay John* is published by Clarkson N. Potter. O'Hagan joins a small writing circle in Victoria.

1960–63    The O'Hagans live on St. Andrew's Street in a house once owned by artist Emily Carr. In 1962, O'Hagan begins writing a regular column, "Then and Now," in the *Islander*, the Victoria *Colonist*'s weekly magazine.

1963–64    *The Woman Who Got On at Jasper Station* is published in 1963 by Alan Swallow, Denver. Margaret O'Hagan is awarded a Canada Council arts grant, and decides to go to Italy, where she had studied mosaic (in Ravenna) in the 1930s. O'Hagan travels to join Margaret in Italy via London, Barcelona, Paris, Rome.

1964–74    The O'Hagans live in Lipari and then in Lingua, both on the Lipari Islands off Messina, Sicily.

1974    O'Hagan returns to Victoria to discover *Tay John* has been reprinted in McClelland and Stewart's New Canadian Library Series. O'Hagan corresponds with George Woodcock, who has written a positive review of the novel for *Maclean's*, and meets P.K. Page; these two are instrumental in having him made an honorary member of the Writers' Union of Canada. Others who support O'Hagan's projects in the last years of his life are Margaret Atwood, Gary Geddes, Robert Harlow, Margaret Laurence, Ken Mitchell, Michael Ondaatje, and Karl Siegler.

1976    O'Hagan is awarded a Canada Council Senior Arts Bursary to write his autobiography.

1977    *The School-Marm Tree* and *The Woman Who Got On at Jasper Station and Other Stories* are published by Talonbooks, Vancouver.

1978    A revised edition of *Wilderness Men* is published by Talonbooks.

1982    O'Hagan receives an honorary doctorate from McGill University; the presentation speech is made by Louis Dudek. O'Hagan dies in September.

# A Letter from Lovat Dickson

Apartment 808
21 Dale Avenue
Toronto, ON
M4W 1K3

7 May 1985

Margery Fee and Chris Petter[1]
University of Victoria
PO Box 1800
Victoria, BC
V8W 3H5

Dear Editors,

I regret not having replied sooner to your letter of 27 March. Yes, I knew Howard O'Hagan, but I have no correspondence or other papers of his; although I believe there may have been a brief exchange of letters when my biography of Grey Owl, *Wilderness Man*, was published in 1973. You could ascertain this by writing to the manuscript division of the Public Archives in Ottawa, who have my papers.[2]

For the four years I was an undergraduate at the University of Alberta, 1923–27, I worked at Jasper Park Lodge during the summer as a chauffeur. Howard's father was the doctor in the then-quite-small town, and I saw Howard frequently during the season. We made some excursions together into the mountains. It was on one of these that I got my finger caught in an overhead cable put up in the old days to give passage over a crevasse. We had to walk back into town, about eight miles. I lost a lot of blood. Howard took me to his father's surgery. Dr. O'Hagan gave me a stiff drink of whiskey, and amputated the finger at the joint.

I did not read Howard's work until I returned to Canada in 1967. I greatly admired it, and am glad to hear that you have his papers. These must include photos, so I need not tell you that he was a very handsome young man, witty and easy to talk to. I think we were about the same age, although as he had already graduated from McGill he may have been a few years older. I wish I could be of more help to you. But this encounter was 60 years ago. I had to work very hard, shovelling gravel at night for the golf course that was being made in order to make overtime pay. Howard used to come and talk to me as I emptied the box cars of this stuff, and entertain me with his conversation.[3] We both had literary ambitions. But don't most people at that age?

Yours sincerely,
Lovat Dickson

NOTES

[1] Chris Petter is the archivist at the University of Victoria.

[2] None of O'Hagan's letters are in this collection.

[3] The idea that Lovat Dickson and Howard O'Hagan had literary conversations beside box cars in the Rockies — indeed, while one of them was slinging gravel — seems somewhat incongruous, given their subsequent careers. Shortly after the last of these conversations, O'Hagan left for Australia and Dickson went to London, and the two lost track of each other for 40 years. Armed with an MA from the University of Alberta, Dickson edited the *Fortnightly Review* in 1929, and the *Review of Reviews* in 1931 and 1932; he ran his own publishing company until 1938. Between 1941 and 1964, he was the general editor and a director of Macmillan and Company. Both O'Hagan and Dickson were fascinated by the figure of the wilderness man, as their overlapping titles make clear (O'Hagan's *Wilderness Men* [1958, 1978]; Dickson's *Wilderness Man: The Strange Story of Grey Owl* [1973]). Both wrote about Grey Owl (Archibald Belaney); Dickson's *Wilderness Man* was written, in part, to correct the picture given in his earlier *Half-Breed: The Story of Grey Owl* (1939), where Grey Owl is presented (as he presented himself) as part Apache. Grey Owl made two highly successful lecture tours of England, one in 1935–36, and the other in 1937–38; not surprisingly, O'Hagan's novel was advertised by his British publisher in 1939 as "A Novel of the Grey Owl Country." Nonetheless, Dickson failed to spot *Tay John*. It is difficult not to speculate about what would have been different for O'Hagan had he sent his novel to Dickson, rather than to Laidlaw and Laidlaw.

# An Interview with
# Howard O'Hagan

### KEITH MAILLARD

When I interviewed Howard O'Hagan in 1979, I was planning to write a book titled "Magic Realism in British Columbia" (or, as I liked to refer to it when I was talking to my friends, "Slug in the Rain"). My second novel was about to be published; I was at work on my third; for the first time since my university days, I had taken to reading literary criticism, and I was filled with the boundless enthusiasm and hubris of the novice. My own literary roots were in the United States; I had only just begun to read Canadian writing, and the territory seemed sparkling fresh to me. I had fallen in love with the province where I lived, and set out to read every work of fiction ever written in British Columbia; I was in search of what I had decided was an indigenous genre: magic realism. With this notion fixed firmly in my mind, I found magical writing under every tree and stone (I was even prepared to call Ethel Wilson's *Swamp Angel* magic realism). When I finally came upon Howard O'Hagan's *Tay John*, I knew I'd hit gold. Here was a big, rough, fascinating, complicated, world-class novel that could easily be incorporated into my critical structure. The more I studied *Tay John*, the better I liked it; I thought it one of the best novels ever written by a Canadian, and I was astonished that O'Hagan was not well known and celebrated from coast to coast.

The novelist Robert Harlow had been a friend of Howard's for years, and arranged for me to interview him. The transcript of our conversation, printed here, preserves Howard's words, but not the essential, compelling, vibrant energy of the man — not his piercing eyes or the rhythm of his delivery, the way he *chose* his words and *placed* them with the exacting care of a master storyteller. A canny reader will certainly notice the struggle going on over topic: I wanted to talk about *Tay John*, but Howard wanted to talk about *The School-Marm Tree* —

and, of course, Howard got his way. But the bare words on the page cannot begin to convey the nuances of the interview — like the delicious moment when Howard pretended that he had forgotten the name of Michael Ondaatje's book: "I have a knife . . ." he began (and then looked up at me with a weirdly impish twinkle to make sure I got it), "I'm learning to turn," he went on in a dry voice, building up the gag for all it was worth. "I think I need to learn to turn it to see certain turns. . . ."

I do not believe that Howard had planned to tell me the tale of the grizzly bear; he was remembering, allowing his mind to wind along its own inner paths; I was held in the increasing tension of the narrative; I focused all of my energy upon him, silently encouraging him to continue. The words "It's hell to grow old" were ripped up out of Howard's guts (I don't know how else to describe it); anyone listening to the tape of the interview will hear a long silence. Both Howard and I had tears in our eyes. When I returned to Vancouver, I dreamed of Howard four nights in a row. In these dreams he said nothing; he simply looked at me.

I never did write the book of literary criticism. In the 14 years since I interviewed Howard, I have become increasingly ignorant, and now know far less than I did then. I certainly don't know enough to write a book titled "Magic Realism in British Columbia," and I don't know whether I would call *Tay John* a work of magic realism or not. The passage of time, however, has not diminished my respect for the book or for the wonderful man who wrote it.

The interview took place on 17 July 1979, in the O'Hagan home in Victoria. For details of publications by and about O'Hagan mentioned in the interview, see Richard Arnold's "Howard O'Hagan: An Annotated Bibliography," which is included in this volume.

KEITH MAILLARD: There seems to be a thread that I'm discovering in people who have written in the province. I just wanted to sort of break it down, and you seem to be the logical place to start.
HOWARD O'HAGAN: Well, actually, most of my writing has not been set in British Columbia but on the east slope of the Rockies.
KM: In Alberta.
HO: Yeah.
KM: I wanted to ask you how you managed to get published in London. Did you have an agent in England?

HO: Yes. It was a chancy proposition. I met someone in Berkeley, California. I was introduced by Margaret Peterson, who is now my wife [to someone who] had the name of this Margaret Watson, and she sold the manuscript of *Tay John* to Laidlaw and Butchart, a very small publishing firm in London. [The company became Laidlaw and Laidlaw shortly before *Tay John* appeared.] This was in 1939. It got top of the column in the literary supplement of the *Times* of London. They said it was a novel that would be long remembered, among other things. And Frank Swinnerton wrote it up in the *Observer* paper, but it received no notice whatever in the United States and very little in Canada. It's still on the shelves, as McClelland and Stewart published it . . .

KM: Yeah, reissued it in 1974.

HO: Yeah. And Clarkson N. Potter in the United States published it in 1960. But I've just written a letter today — or, at least the Writers' Union of Canada sent me a letter that they suggested I send to McClelland and Stewart — because the novel is being taught in universities across the country, so I am told. And I haven't had one single cent in royalties from it.

KM: From the M and S edition?

HO: No, no. Nothing. [See Margery Fee's "A Note on the Publishing History of Howard O'Hagan's *Tay John*," which is part of this volume.]

KM: That's terrible.

HO: Yeah.

KM: How did you come to write it?

HO: Well, that I really don't know.

KM: Let me try the question a different way. Is there a specific kind of book you were planning to write, or was it something you just felt you had to do?

HO: No, I don't know. Milton and Cheadle wrote *The North-West Passage by Land*. They went across Canada on the route now taken by the Canadian National through Yellowhead Pass and down. And they damn near starved to death. They had to eat their horses. And they found a skeleton by a fire — by the remains of a fire. The skeleton had no head. And they searched everywhere for the head, but they couldn't find it. So I started this book as a diary by the man who had lost his head, you know. And I wrote the first four chapters on that. And I saw it didn't work, so I rewrote the first chapter, and the second, third, and fourth stayed as they were. But I had no prevision of what the book was going to be at all.

KM: When did you start writing? Was that at McGill, or had you started writing earlier?

HO: Oh, I had done writing — I was a sports reporter for the *Montreal Star*, editor in chief of the *McGill Daily*, then on the *Edmonton Journal* I covered the northern beat. And I wrote columns for the *Sydney Morning Herald*. I had my first story published in Sydney, Australia. It wasn't much of a story. It was set in the South Seas and was about the first mate and a Chinese cook and the cat. [See "How It Came About," in this volume.]

KM: Had you always wanted to write a novel, or did this one sneak up on you?

HO: I really can't say whether I wanted to write a novel or not. I was doing it. You've read the novel, I guess?

KM: Uh huh.

HO: When I finished the first part, its utterance was faintly biblical . . . mainly. When I got to the end of the fourth chapter, I saw I couldn't go on with this omniscient . . .

KM: Narrator?

HO: Yeah. And I was out walking in the hills behind Berkeley, California, where you overlook San Francisco Bay and can see the fog coming in on a summer day — beautiful sight — pouring through the Golden Gate. And Jack Denham, which was the name of the marine reporter of the *San Francisco Chronicle* — a man whom I had never met — began to talk to me while I was up there alone. You know, as crazy as this sounds, apocryphal I know, it's so. And I got back to my flat in Berkeley about five o'clock, and I was just full of this but I always worked in the morning and I was determined that I wouldn't start on it until the next morning. I spent a sleepless night, and it was as though this thing had been (this is the fifth chapter, "The Bare Foot") . . . as though I were just copying something down. Samuel Taylor Coleridge started to write *Kubla Khan* after he had had an anodyne, and he woke up with this thing right before his eyes and started to copy it down. And he was interrupted by a man on business who held him in conversation for an hour or so, and when he came back there was nothing left to write. . . .

[There was] a group of us in Berkeley — they were professors. Most of them had PhDs. I just have a BA, LLB. Each man, once a month (we met once a month), had to write the minutes. I was chosen this particular time, and it was just about Mr. Blizzard and Mr. Weatherweary — the dialogue between these two. [See E.W. Strong's "The Berkeley Arts

Club: Chronicles by and of Howard O'Hagan," in this volume.] One of the professors asked me how I did it. He said he couldn't imagine. I said if I knew how I did it I could never do it. And it's the same with writing in general, as distinct from articles.

KM: Yes. I know the feeling you're talking about. I've had it, too, when the story comes and it tells itself, and you feel almost like you're an empty vessel and the story is just pouring right through you.

HO: That's right.

KM: All I find I can do after that is revise it and tighten it up, but I can't change it because I didn't write it. It came from somewhere else.

HO: No, that's right. Very good. The pieces I've had published — short stories and so on — I've rewritten four or five times.

KM: What sorts of things did you like to read? What other novelists were you reading, or had you read?

HO: Oh, well, W.H. Hudson, *Far Away and Long Ago*, and Cunningham Graham White, who wrote about the Argentine. It was very odd. I should have read them because I went down to the Argentine to become [chief of publicity for the] *Ferrocaril Central Argentino*. It's an English-owned railroad. . . . Oh, and I read Joseph Conrad. I'm not a great reader. There are lots of things I haven't read that I should have read. [The Book of] Ecclesiastes has always interested me. It has no real place in the Bible, as far as I can make out, but it's a beautiful job.

KM: Yeah, I remember reading something by someone who wasn't sure how Ecclesiastes made it into the Bible because it is so different from the rest of the book.

HO: Yes.

KM: So how long did it take you to write *Tay John*? Was the rest of the writing like that — very fast, automatic writing?

HO: No. No, there are a lot of things in *Tay John* I wish I'd never written at all. For instance, he has just one hand. Have you ever tried to put a bridle on a horse with one hand? No, it's impossible. . . . But my interest right now is not so much in *Tay John*. . . . *The School-Marm Tree* is a simple sort of story. George Woodcock wrote it up in a review in the *Times* of Victoria. He complained that the characters were types. Of course they were types. So are Shakespeare's characters types. Dickens's too. And he said the plot, well you would see it stretching ahead of you. Of course. I mean what's a plot? A plot — you remember the clothes hangers they used to have in the old days standing in the hall or whatnot? that you hang your things on? a pole with hooks? Well, that's what a plot is. A pole with hooks. It's not interesting itself at all. It depends what's hung upon it. But George Woodcock made no such concession. He spoke highly of the work generally, and he liked the short stories especially. He compared them to Camus and Sartre. But you know when you write a book you just set yourself up as a target. You have to accept what's coming.

KM: Yeah, I know.

HO: And it doesn't really matter to me so much. But this *School-Marm* is a story whose theme . . . is the same theme as *Maria Chapdelaine* by Louis Hémon, a Frenchman, who died in a speeder accident on what was then the Canadian Northern in northern Ontario. And it's the same theme as *Wild Geese* by Martha Ostenso, except that both these heroines . . . had their attention fixed on the United States as the place to go, whereas my character, Selva, has — she's in the mountains — her attention riveted on Montreal or an eastern Canadian city. But it's essentially the same. They're trying to get away from where they are and to go somewhere where life is.

KM: The interesting thing to me about *The School-Marm Tree* was that you had written from a woman's point of view, which seemed very different from *Tay John*. Did you find that hard to do?

HO: No, I didn't find it hard to do. No, we had George Woodcock again. He says he found it impossible that a girl like Selva who had been just a maid in someone's house should take charge of a dude ranch in the mountains. Well, we had a girl like Selva in the house for four years. She used to do all the shopping. At first my mother kept track of the accounts, but after that she didn't. We had eight or twelve people in to dinner, and this girl Mitzi attended to everything. She looked after the shopping, she did the washing. It was slave work. Twenty-five dollars a month. Well, I have been a guide in the Rocky Mountains for many, many years off and on, and I took charge one summer of a dude ranch in the foothills near Brulé, just east of Jasper. And I had a good cook, that was the main thing. When you're out on the trail in the mountains with tourists, your horses come first, but here on this dude ranch I had to keep these people occupied from half past seven or eight in the morning until ten or eleven at night, and this just drove me half cuckoo. They weren't interested in me or in the country — that is, most of them. They were interested in talking to one another about hotels where they both stayed or almost stayed, you know — exchanging credentials. We were just servants, and I remember taking one couple in — this was the time of Roosevelt's presidency in the United States — and they spoke to me of the cripple in the White House and I said "your president is very highly regarded up here." They cancelled the reservation. They had to stay one night, anyway. And I took them back to the railroad station the next morning. They didn't think that a mere guide should have an opinion.

KM: You shouldn't have been expressing an opinion about the president?

HO: No.

KM: The one tourist who seems to come off fairly sympathetically is the mountaineer. His name's Branchflower?

HO: Oh, yes.

KM: Most of them don't come off too well. But he comes off fairly well. He comes up and he climbs the mountain and makes a pass at Selva and then he goes home.

HO: Yes, he tried to make a pass at Selva. I don't think he did, did he?

KM: Well, she didn't go to his cabin. She says to him . . .

HO: Oh yeah, that's right. And you know why I pulled that out? This girl was typing it for me in a college just on the edge of Duncan near Cowichan Bay. She said "I think, Mr. O'Hagan, that would destroy my conception of Selva." So I cut it out.

KM: Oh — on the original draft Selva went?

HO: Yeah. [The typist] didn't want to copy it out.

KM: I was thinking about the two books together in my mind. In *Tay John*, there are only two women — there's the wife . . .

HO: The wife of Swamas, the Indian woman.

KM: Oh, I had completely forgotten the Indian woman.

HO: I thought she was pretty good. But the other women in *Tay John* are terrible. Just terrible.

KM: You mean terribly drawn or terrible people?

HO: Terribly drawn.

KM: You think so?

HO: Yeah.

KM: I thought the wife, Julia Alderson, was well drawn, because you paint her very quickly and you can see her very quickly. She has her high-heeled riding boots on, and there's a very quick description of her, but the picture comes quite alive — her chubby hands, that is the one detail. As a character she seems quite real to me. I had a little trouble with Ardith Aeriola.

HO: I had trouble with both of them. They don't seem to me to be agreeable at all. I mean this Alderson woman comes into the clearing where Tay John is, and her perfume — well it pervades her, it pervades the place. First of all, that's no way to perfume. And secondly, it wouldn't prevail over the smell of horse.

KM: But the effect that both those women have on the plot is . . . the feeling I had was that it was a very male world with all these men around; McLeod has a picture of a woman on his wall in his cabin just sort of like a vision or a dream. When the real women appear, the whole focus of attention is turned on them, and of course they both cause the plot to happen. It seemed very interesting to me that, having looked at women from that point of view, you should later write another book from inside a woman's mind — *The School-Marm Tree.*

HO: That's because I didn't get inside the women's minds at all in *Tay John*, except for the Indian woman, Hanni, who was dying. And she said, "Speak to me loudly, for my head lies on a river." I think that's a beautiful line. I don't know where in the hell it came from.

KM: It is a beautiful line. Was any of the material in *Tay John* based on your personal knowledge of Indians or Indian myth?

HO: No. Well, of course Tête Jaune was an Iroquois half-breed who had a cache west of what is now Jasper at the juncture of the Swiftwater and the Fraser. He was a trapper and a hunter. But the myth of Tay John's birth is from the Carrier Indians near where what is now Prince George. It was written up by Diamond Jenness, and I think the title is *The Indians of Canada*, but I'm not sure. Anyway, I wrote [Jenness] and told him that I was writing a book and I would like to use this in it. Of course, I didn't need to ask permission because, after all, happenings aren't copyrighted. It's only the writing that's patented. And it's my writing — it's not his writing. But anyway, he wired me that I was welcome to it. So that's about as far as the actual Indian myths concerned me, but I went into Vancouver because instead of calling these people, you know, Broken Knee, or Sitting Bull, or whatnot, I wanted their actual names. And I went to the University of British Columbia to see a professor of anthropology. Damn, but I forget his name now [it was Charles Hill-Tout; see Ralph Maud's "Ethnographic Notes on Howard O'Hagan's *Tay John*," which is included in this volume]. He gave me the names that I've used, which was very decent of him. I think the anthropologists, people who have really studied the Indians, look with some disdain on a man who is an outsider and has

28

only a casual knowledge of it. But I've worked with half-breeds on the trail (that's a horrible term — half-breed), and I've heard them maligned and I have found them impeccably honest all the way through. I remember one evening — and of course in those days (60 years ago) they couldn't go into the liquor store — this man . . . Plante, who was half Cree and half French Canadian, was [drunk], and he fancied the neckerchief that I was wearing, which was worth probably 50¢. He said he would give me his bridle for it. And his bridle was rolled, with a curbed bit, and worth probably $25 or $30. The next morning I said "Isaac . . . you were pretty drunk last night, weren't you." He said, "Yes, Howard, I was pretty drunk." I said, "Look, this bridle is worth money." He said, "That neckerchief you're wearing isn't worth anything, so let's just exchange things and put them back where they were." And he spoke perfect English. At another time, when I was managing this dude ranch, I took a very well-known Edmonton lawyer and politician and his wife to visit Isaac at his teepee. And there were drums sounding in the foothills. Very impressive sound. It seems to come through the ground. I've heard it in Fiji too. And this man spoke pidgin English to Isaac.

KM: The people around there would be what — Shuswap?

HO: No, there were half-breed Crees that lived between Fish Lake near Brulé and 200 miles north on the Smoky River at a place called Grand Cache where they went in the wintertime. In the spring and summer they were near Fish Lake, near Brulé. But they weren't true Indians. No, the Shuswaps are a branch of the Salish tribe who settled just under Mount Robson. Most feudal campground I've seen anywhere. Milton and Cheadle encountered them there. And there were a couple of them working for Fred Brewster's outfit, for which I was working. I was at Jasper. They were very different than the Crees. They were a short, squat people. The Crees were generally tall and slender. . . .

We were living in Lucerne — my mother and father and me and my sister. There was an old trapper across Yellowhead Lake. . . . This old man — he was about 60, a youngster to me now (I'm 77) — and these mountain goats were over on the north side of the Seven Sisters, which is a range above a lake. And just before the first snow came, two or three days before, the goats would come over onto the south side of the mountain because they have sort of a built-in barometer. They knew what was coming. And they would trickle down through the gulleys of the Seven Sisters. There were about 40 or 50 of them, and they were as white as snow. They'd shed their winter coats, and they were growing new, and they were as white as the snow, whose harbingers they were. And Daniel MacNamara [the old trapper] would go up to the trap line, and he took me on one of these occasions. Before taking me up, he described to me what it was like above his cabin, which was really like a doghouse when I got to it. He described the pools up in the alp lands of water where the caribou came down to drink. And they were as blue as the sky. I saw them. They were like pieces of sky fallen down into the alp lands. The old guy was illiterate, but he had this feeling — although it was a tough life as a trapper — for his environment.

I had been out with George Hargreaves, who was a great bear hunter in his time. Grizzly bear. And we were going up a torrent of a creek coming down into the Canoe River off the west slopes of the Rockies. Under the lee of rocks that gathered up out of the ice of the creek there were beautiful ice flowers. You know, when you're on snowshoes you carry a staff. And George would say to me, "Howard, those things are sure well put together," and then he would knock on the piece with his stick — with his staff.

And there was Jack Brewster. Brewster founded the guiding business in Banff near the turn of the century, and in Jasper in about 1910. And Jack Brewster was internationally known as a goat hunter. Now, goat are much more difficult to hunt than sheep. I've been within 14 or 15 feet of a goat. He lives in craggy places above the alp land, and the sheep live on the alp land between the timber and the crags and ice. Jack Brewster sometimes would have a hunter who wanted to bag a goat, and Jack Brewster tested them because you had to climb higher, and so on and so forth. He said they're like old men — he was speaking of them in the spring — like old men going around in their winter underwear. And Jack once . . . spied a grizzly bear digging after a gopher, and he had his shoulders right down into it. Well, anyway, I think this was a mistake that Jack made as a hunter. He had the tourist [he was escorting] shoot the bear, and, because the bear was down there, the tourist shot him through his kidneys and lungs. The bear took shelter in a belt of spruce, and of course Jack had to go after him. When he approached this thicket, the bear charges out. Jack was down on one knee, and his rifle misfired, and he could see this bear coming at him with his open mouth streaming blood. But Jack had been followed by his second guide . . . who shot the grizzly not through the heart because the grizzly would still come on them, but he broke his neck. And Jack told me, he said "Howard, I had blood on my left boot, he was so close, the grizzly." He was the most man I've ever seen in one package in my life. He died of cancer of the oesophagus. He drank a lot of — well, we all did on the trail, I guess — very hot tea. Ten cups. That may have been the cause of it, I don't know. But anyway, he was just a skeleton when he died. It's hell to grow old, you know, in a way. All these men are dead before you. You miss them so much. I miss men more than I do women. . . . Well, I don't think I've given you very much, but I hope it will be some help.

KM: Oh, you've given me plenty, you've given me a lot of good things. You've just got me thinking now about some of the images of violence in both your books, and they're very sudden, and they're quite extreme, and they seem to me quite realistic. I think you intended them to be. Did you?

HO: I don't think one has any intention, you know. Again, aside from articles, then you have an intention. No, one only sees what he's going to write when he's written it. At least that's been my experience — in what I regard as my good writing. That isn't true of all of *Tay John*. I think *The School-Marm Tree* is better written as a whole.

KM: Did you know that Tay John was going to cut his hand off at the point that he did, or did that just happen when you were writing?

HO: It was part . . . well it could have happened to me. I don't know of anyone who's cut off his hand — actually tried to cut off his hand. It's pretty difficult to [do], you know. You could do it all right.

KM: You would really have to have a hell of a wallop.

HO: Yeah.

♦ ♦ ♦

KM: Another series of images that stays with me is at the beginning of *Tay John*: Red Rorty gets burnt up by the Indians, and they put a stone in his mouth — he's a skeleton with a stone still in his mouth. At the end of the book, Tay John vanishes into the snow, dragging the body of the woman; her mouth is full of snow. Again, in *The School-Marm Tree*, the Englishman is hurt in the fight with Slim. It's his mouth that's hurt. His mouth fills up with blood because his tongue is cut. And, just thinking about these three images, it seems almost as though speech is very difficult; it is very difficult to say anything.

HO: Well I never thought of that, but I consider speech difficult, yes.

31

KM: I mean particularly in terms of the landscape where this action takes place. The landscape is so awesome and overpowering that when you come to speak about it it's almost as though the snow silences you. The landscape itself silences you and makes it difficult or impossible to speak at all. I suppose all of us who write fiction end up trying to write about things that you can't write about, but you write about them anyway.

HO: What do you mean?

KM: You do the best you can. The feelings, the emotions that cause the writing to happen — somehow you can never get them on the page, so you just do the best you can, but it's never as intense as you felt it. Do you know what I mean?

◆ ◆ ◆

KM: I'm originally from West Virginia.

HO: Oh, are you? I've never been down that far. Maryland is as far south as I've gone — California, I mean, down as far as Los Angeles. It's a hell of a place.

KM: Los Angeles?

HO: Yeah.

KM: I didn't like it. I worked there for a while. I didn't like it at all.

HO: Terrible. The air was god-awful.

KM: Too fast. But I went back to West Virginia this summer, and one of the people I saw was my grandmother. She's 93. Some of her memories are amazing. She said something very similar to what you've just said, which is that almost everyone she was close to and she grew up with are gone, and she's the last one.

HO: Yeah, it's lonely. I have a chap coming to see me on Monday I knew in the Argentine 40 years ago. I don't know why he wants to come over to see me. We have absolutely nothing in common. . . .

KM: The real south is strange. It's hard to understand unless you've lived there or you've grown up there. Some people think Faulkner makes it up, but he doesn't. It's true. It's the way it is. It's the way it was when he was writing about it.

HO: Faulkner was an outstanding writer, no doubt about that. Hemingway, I don't think he's so much of a writer. People can write in the style of Hemingway. No one except Faulkner can write like Faulkner. . . . The year Faulkner got the Nobel Prize, Hemingway said "I would prefer to have worked on 'The Old Man and the Sea' than to have got the Nobel Prize." What a petty thing to say. And of course he wouldn't.

KM: Of course not.

HO: And his breast-beating to make himself a man. I've known other writers who are the same way. They make a profession of being a man. I don't know. That seems to me what you more or less take for granted.

KM: Yeah. Ernest really worked that way. He overdid it.

HO: I think some of his short stories are stupendous. I don't know if stupendous is the right word or not. The two killers who come into this sort of restaurant — lunch place — and carry on a conversation. I knew two men just like that in Vancouver when I was down and out. Believe me, I was down and out, and I answered this advertisement. [An employer] wanted canvassers or something or other. I went [to see him and was told that] the idea was you were to call people up and you would get money for a church or something like that. Of course [the employer] would get the money. And two Vancouver detectives came. They just barged into his house. They had no search warrant. And I told them, I said, "these men have no right here. Tell them to get out. There's no search warrant. I'm a graduate of law." They carried on this conversation just like Ernest Hemingway . . . concerning this guy and what they could do to him. They couldn't do anything to him.

◆ ◆ ◆

HO: I used to write a thousand words in the morning between nine and twelve or one. Now it's down to about 300. I'm trying to write about my early days in the Rockies. It's coming pretty damn hard. But you know a writer has a wonderful privilege. He can live his life twice.

KM: Yeah, I've found that true myself. People ask me how I can remember certain things; I have a great memory for details because I'm sitting writing about them.

HO: When I was five or six years old in the Crowsnest Pass in Southern Alberta [our maid] used to take me for walks, and brought me in this night and showed me a little barn owl . . . and showed me the first crocus of the spring. It was like a chalice of snow, and I saw water running down . . . put my hand out to grab it . . . first of the season.

KM: You studied under Leacock.

HO: What a wonderful guy he was. I guess he didn't like the Irish. "*Mr.*

*O'Hagan*, your handwriting is painstaking enough in its way, but it has a peculiar cussedness." My handwriting was bad. In law school, the professor gave up trying to read it and asked me to read my paper to him. . . . If I had read all my papers [aloud] I think I would have got better than second-class honours. It's always [been] second-class honours.

♦ ♦ ♦

KM: In the little introduction that P.K. Page wrote to *The School-Marm Tree* . . .

HO: It was pretty good, wasn't it?

KM: Yes, it was. She said you were talking about a presence in the mountains. Could you talk a little about that?

HO: Well, it's very hard to talk about that. I fully notice it when I've been alone in the wintertime. And it would seem that there was someone keeping time with my snowshoes, just off a distance. I couldn't see him. But this has been better portrayed than I could ever do it by a French-Canadian writer whose name I've forgotten [in a poem] called, as I remember, "The Walker on the Snow." It's set in a canyon north of Montreal or Quebec, I forget. When men went through that canyon, they felt this presence, or they heard this man snowshoeing in unison with them. The faster they went, the faster he kept up with them. I think it was "The Walker of the Snow." It was a very moving poem. But now, you know, the yippies and peace and god knows whatnot have taken over places like the Thompson Valley. . . . There are hundreds of them now. We used to go in there with horses, and we'd be the only people there except possibly a park warden, and we had the silence and the flies and mosquitoes, too, to ourselves. But now these people are so poorly bred they have made a devastation of this beautiful, beautiful valley on its . . .

KM: Its northern face, isn't it?

HO: Southern. They are so precipitous that in the wintertime they are still black. They don't hold the snow. . . . These people have no respect for silence or the rivers running or anything. Why the hell do they go in there at all? I don't know. One has not the authority to keep them out, but there must be some way to discourage them. They destroy the valleys for other people.

KM: Edmund Wilson once said that most Americans look on Canada

34

as a playground that, luckily, is situated directly to the north. Well, in some sense, aren't the people you're talking about just modern versions of the tourists who came up to Jasper? There are more of them now. There's a similar kind of disregard for the environment.

HO: No. The people I took out (this is before the highway was through — I think the highway people are much the same as these hippies, or whatever they're called), with one or two exceptions, they had high respect for the mountains and everything that went on, and they were full of questions. Too many for me to answer. But these other creatures, they don't ask any questions. They think they know it all.

KM: Now, probably, the presence of the highway makes things too easy. The thought of having to walk or ride on horseback into the bush immediately discourages a large number of people. And if you can just drive there, it's too easy.

HO: But they've destroyed what they've come to see.

◆ ◆ ◆

KM: Can I ask you something about the reception that *Tay John* had? You said it was reviewed in the *Observer* and the *Times*.

HO: Yes, it was the literary supplement of the *Times* of London. The top of a column. The book didn't sell worth a damn.

KM: But was there any notice taken of it in Canada?

HO: Very little. The *Edmonton Journal* and the Vancouver *Province* were the ones I remember. But I didn't subscribe to a clipping bureau, so I don't know.

KM: Did you meet anyone because of *Tay John*? Did anyone come around and talk to you after that?

HO: No. No one showed any interest in *Tay John* at all until about four years ago. We had just come back from Sicily, and we went out to lunches and dinners and whatnot, and people were talking about *Tay John*. Of course, they hadn't read *Tay John*, but they were looking forward to reading it. Anyway, I wondered what sparked this interest. . . . When I learned about George Woodcock having put two or three paragraphs [about *Tay John* in *Maclean's*; see Arnold D12], I wrote him to tell him why I was surprised, and so on. He wrote me back that he was not the only one who admired *Tay John*, there was Michael Ondaatje, and he sent me Michael's article in *Canadian Literature* [see Arnold C9].

35

KM: You met Ondaatje?

HO: Oh yes.

KM: Very nice fellow.

HO: Oh, he's a wonderful chap. Thank god there's only one of him.

KM: What do you mean?

HO: Well, I think two would be too much to handle. . . . Yes, he was here a few weeks ago or maybe a few months after that. He sent me his latest book of poems. I have a knife. I'm learning to turn . . . I think I need to learn to turn it to see certain turns . . . [*There's a Trick with a Knife I'm Learning to Do*, 1979].

KM: Did you read his novel? He wrote a novel called *Coming through Slaughter*. It was quite good.

HO: Yes. I didn't think so much of that. In the case of a lot of this modern poetry I feel very much like an outsider. I don't participate in what's happening. I observe it. For instance, "We were the first, to ever burst," no, "The fair breeze blew, the white foam flew . . . We were the first that ever burst / Into that silent sea" [O'Hagan quotes from Samuel Taylor Coleridge's *The Rime of the Ancient Mariner*]. Now I'm part of that. I am a fellow sharer. But much of the modern poetry that I read seems to be — well it leaves me cold. It seems to be a form of — what's the word — a form of self-indulgence.

KM: Well, I've decided not to write about poetry because I don't understand it. I read some modern poetry, but the only thing I think I'm competent to comment on is fiction, because I write it and understand how it's done.

HO: Well, my problem is people come and give me books of poems and I'm supposed to write letters about them. Am I not?

KM: Do you mean for a grant application, or a review?

HO: No, but I'm supposed to write and tell them what I thought of it. And very often I don't think anything at all. But now, take P.K. Page's poems. That's a different matter. What she's writing about — except in the first, in her early poems — is not entirely a personal experience. It's something that embraces the audience, it seems to me. Anyway, some of her poems take me right out of myself.

KM: Let me ask you about some other writers. Have you read Hubert Evans's *Mist on the River*?

HO: No, I haven't.

KM: How about *The Double Hook* by Sheila Watson?

HO: *The Double Hook* by whom?

KM: Sheila Watson.

HO: I probably haven't read most of these books that you mention. No, I'd like to read — I haven't read it yet — *The Stone Angel* by Margaret Laurence.

KM: Oh, it's good.

HO: I've read her stories about Manitoba ("The Loon," I think), and I think they're magnificent.

KM: Did you ever read Malcolm Lowry?

HO: I've read him and I've met him.

KM: Tell me about that.

HO: I think he's a great writer, but he is a miserable little bastard. First of all, he's not a Canadian, anyway. So I don't see why he should be regarded as a Canadian writer. He's an English writer.

KM: That's true.

HO: His attitude was the usual British attitude towards Canadians, you know. Colonial, still. [A.J.M.] Smith introduced us.

KM: Where was this?

HO: In Vancouver. We were drinking beer in the Hotel Vancouver, and then we went out to Lowry's place on the North Island.

KM: Dollarton?

HO: Yeah. Before that, Lowry more or less took command of the conversation, and he was speaking about the hardships and whatnot of being an ordinary seaman. Well, I'd been an ordinary seaman in the South Pacific, and it's one of the dullest jobs I've ever done, aside from digging ditches. I've done that as well. When we got out to their place [Smith], Margaret [O'Hagan], and Lowry's wife — the American newspaper woman [Margerie Bonner Lowry] — left Malcolm and me, and we went down to the dining room, and he said to me then (or he'd said it earlier), that [Smith] had given him a copy of *Tay John*, and he said that he thought some of the descriptive passages were quite good. I said I thought some of his descriptive passages were quite good, too, but I wondered if descriptive passages had any place in a novel. I cited Tolstoy. The only descriptive passage of his I remembered is when . . . [Prince Andrei, in *War and Peace*], was going to make his call on Count Rostov, and going there he sees this big oak tree. It's in its winter garb, which is to say it has no garb at all — it's bare. And he's just lost his wife and that's what life seems like to him. Then he goes there and he sees this young girl . . . [Natasha]. He stands at his window and he hears these two girls talking below him, and one says "Well it's late, I'm wanting to go in," and Natasha says "No, I want to watch the stars," or something like that. And he hears this lovely voice. He returns to this place, and he's full of emotion for this girl, and he sees the tree — well this is six weeks later — and all the leaves are out. It's life beginning again. Now that's real descriptive writing. Some of mine is description for its own sake. There's no [spirit of] place there at all.

KM: So what did Lowry say when you told him that?

HO: I don't think he had anything very much to say. Oh yes, he wanted to arm wrestle. I put him down. It was a cinch.

# How It Came About

HOWARD O'HAGAN

*"How It Came About" was first published
in the Sydney* Mail, *27 July 1927.*

She was ordinary enough to look at, the tramp steamer Argus, 6000 tons, bound from 'Frisco to Sydney; altogether her black, bulging bows, her short, black funnel set a bit aft of the white bridgework, gave her an air of squatness. She seemed to have been placed on the waters and shoved down into them, and because her forepart was a good deal higher than her stern she had the semblance of trying, in a futile sort of way, to climb out again.

That, indeed, was the only impression of animation that she offered. Otherwise she appeared to be held with ropes of iron to some implacable end, to some excessive purpose, as she kept her course through the soft swell of the blue Pacific one December. Twice at night a ship had passed, swinging at first out of the darkness like a lantern held in unsteady hands, finally to take the form of a toy vessel lighted with candles plying a remote and wavering course in an interminable blackness.

Thus for long days of monotony the Argus journeyed over the seas, caught between two unalterable horizons, with the ocean sobbing its immemorial anguish at her bows, her smoke lying a stream of dusk across the leaden sky, and her wake reaching out from the unseen coast she had left as though to restrain her from the destiny towards which she was led.

Yet she was a living symbol of the fate of men she held within her vibrating frame — voyagers between the impenetrable horizons of two infinities, with lives of obscure designs and unspoken ambitions, begun

39

in the four corners of the earth and thrown together for this one passage over the Pacific to partake of common hardship, common peril, and infrequent consolation in the individual solving of the puzzle of a few years, allotted from the boundless store of time, to be the substance of their respective existences. More than that, in her bosom she carried a deep and smouldering discontent, born of the hates of men. Not that it was wholly evident, not even to the mate, Mr. Singleton, whom it should have affected vitally — but then "vitally" is not the word. The right word is not in our language.

It came about in this manner. Near the close of a calm, hot day, just off the port quarter lay Lone Tree Island — Lone Tree Island that, between Hawaii and Fiji, seems to lie on the very surface of the waters with an atmosphere of aged tranquillity about it. A line of white, like a fringe of snow, marks the break of the surf that has beat upon its shore for centuries past the understanding of man.

The heat was still to be felt. It was so hot, in fact, that Mr. Singleton on the bridge fancied that the very ocean must have gained heat from the sun which fell quickly towards the skyline beyond the bows. That it would steam and sizzle from this dull red ball that, like a hot coal, seemed to sink right into it. That it would boil.

He was peering about under lowered brows as he paced up and down with a heavy, exaggerated tread. He brought his heels down very determinedly, as if he were pushing tacks in with them. A stocky, dark man with a head that jutted out from his wide shoulders like the bowsprit of a sailing vessel, and with eyes that protruded somewhat, giving the notion that they had been partially forced out of their sockets, as by a cord tied about his head and tightened, pulled very tight. His hands behind his back, his body leaning a bit forward, he communicated a feeling of bad temper. This may have arisen because of the sticky day, or it may have been aimed, for some dim reason, at Captain Burrows, that conscience of the ship, who was below, as was his habit except in bad weather, when he was needed. It was no secret to the crew that the two did not get on very well.

Yes, the mate was in an ugly temper. Even Ah Lee, the only Chinaman on board, who was doing a short spell at the wheel, felt that — Ah Lee, who stood a grey figure of immobility, like a piece of granite, with his eyes as the one feature in his make-up to distinguish him as something alive. And they were glazed, as though his mind had left his body and was winging its way many miles ahead of the ship. His movements as

40

he ceaselessly caught and turned the spokes of the wheel were no part of him. They were separate, distinct.

It was then that the kitten came up the ladder. Emitting a faint, barely perceptible "me-ow," it walked slowly over to Ah Lee, its grey tail curving in the air. The Oriental took his eyes off the oscillating pointer for a moment to stoop down and scratch the back that was rubbing against his ankle.

"Keep your eye on the course. Never mind the cat. Chop, chop! You savee?" Singleton snapped out at him abruptly, very abruptly. And then, for no ostensible reason at all, added: "I'll show you, you yellow mongrel."

With that he stalked over and grasped the kitten — it was only the size of a squirrel — in his hand and pitched it, literally hurled it into the sea. It was as sudden as that. Ah Lee made no comment. It was not in his nature to do so. He remained as imperturbable as the most rigorous traditions of his race could demand.

Nevertheless from the corner of his eye he saw the grey thing curve high in the air before splashing into the waves a bit astern of amidships. That was all. Just one splash, a ripple that lasted a bare second before it was swallowed with hasty arrogance by the swirl of the ship. That one small furrow on the face of those waters was to remain for many days in the vision of Ah Lee. That, too, was his nature and that of his people.

The Chinaman was not the only one to perceive what had occurred. Macklin, the second mate, a slim, red-faced young man with a slight moustache and tousled fair hair, came rushing on to the bridge from his post aft, where he had been tending the davits of one of the lifeboats. He wore a scowl.

"Rather a rotten trick, wasn't it, Singleton?" he blurted right out, ignoring the formality of "Mr." His blue eyes glared, so far as it was in their power to do so. He was a compassionate man, Macklin.

"The Chink" — nodding towards Ah Lee — "thought a lot of that kitten. And you knew — we all know — that he fed it and let it sleep in his bunk." The object of his tirade look no notice whatever. Singleton stood, with his back turned, watching the sun pull with it from the surface of the waters its many-hued carpet of colours as it dropped into the underworld.

Macklin went on, almost conversationally: "My little girl in Sydney had one once. It was killed. A car killed it. It means a great deal to lose

41

something like that. It was a rotten thing to do, anyway," he finished with sudden vehemence; and then, a bit discomposed by the other's attitude of indifference, he left the bridge, swearing softly to himself.

I heard him later speaking to the Captain about it. They were together on the bridge, and Macklin was looking up at his superior, who was quite a tall man, with black features, accentuated by a stubby black moustache and eyes set so close into a prominent nose that their colour was lost. The two speakers were just an indistinct splotch of murk, and the sounds that emanated from them seemed startlingly trivial in the silver-lustre of the night. It was two nights after what we had come to mention as "Singleton's indiscretion."

"Took it up and threw it over as he would the core of an apple," Macklin was saying. "I saw it all from where I was aft. The poor little brute hit the waves almost beneath me, right under my nose, so to speak. Singleton hates Chinamen; that was his way of showing it."

Captain Burrows, who for reasons of his own had previously refrained from all reference to the affair, being in addition a man to whom comment, except in the most urgent circumstances, was distasteful, studied Macklin thoughtfully, so I gathered from the period of silence before venturing a reply calculated to turn the conversation into other channels.

"Have you noticed the crew lately, Macklin?" he asked in his measured, sonorous voice. "They seem a bit restless. I saw that big low-haired Swedish fellow talk back to Singleton this morning. No mumbling either; he came right out with it. It was about the port anchor: Singleton was trying to show him something about it, and he answered that he learned that a long time ago, before Singleton ever thought about it."

"That's the whole point of it, sir," the other put in. "It's that kitten business cropping up again. That creature, believe it or not, was the one connecting link between the rest of the crew and the Chink. He was very fond of it, you know, and they to seem to take that as a proof of his humanity. It made them feel that they had something in common. It's not that they mind losing the kitten, but they resent any interference in their relations with one another. That's what it amounts to."

"Perhaps." The Captain moved his body uneasily. "But ——"

Macklin interrupted: "They feel they have had something taken away from them — that's how I size it up. I came across that fellow Ingram, the little American, talking to the Chinaman. 'Heap no good first mate

Charlie,' he was saying. They all call Ah Lee 'Charlie.' The Chinaman, of course, didn't reply. It seems they have lost all contact with him. Not that that would matter, except they once had it. On top of that they — well, they always respected Singleton; but then you know how it is, sir — they are apt to regard him differently now."

Macklin's tendency to criticise the mate did not appear to meet with much favour, as Burrows responded rather shortly: "Oh, I don't believe it will amount to very much." Then, turning away, and seeming to make the statement to himself, he added: "I would like to find out what has come over Singleton lately. He's been confoundedly irritable — moody."

It was a question that perhaps Singleton himself could not answer. Certainly no one else could, any more than it could have been told whence he came, where his people were, if he had any, or what his ideas were. He was extraordinarily self-contained, living within himself and solely for himself. Not at all like Macklin, for instance, who made no secret of his longing to return to his home in Sydney, where his wife and young daughter lived, waiting for him.

One imagined them in a small white cottage with a green lawn, and probably a straight pebble path leading from the trim gate to the doorway. It would be like the second mate. This voyage he had stated, would be his last — for a time, at any rate.

"I'll stay home and potter around the garden a bit. Plant some creepers and trees. I've brought a California orange tree with me this trip. And then in the afternoons we can go down to the beach," he had confided to me during the second watch one night. He concluded with his usual "you know," which, always accompanied by a sharp turn of the head towards the person addressed, more resembled a gesture than an expression.

So for the remainder of the voyage, until it finished in Sydney two weeks later, the incident of the kitten faded into an obscurity from which it emerged occasionally when some casual action aroused its memory. Two constant symptoms, however, were evident.

The first was the conciliatory position that the crew took up in regard to Ah Lee. It was as though, being of the same colour as the mate, they sensed that they were involved in his wrong and anxious to make amends. One might say, for want of a better word, that they were "polite" to the Chinaman. Not so polite, however, as to use his own name in preference to "Charlie," this being the one vestige of contempt for his race of which they could not rid themselves. As for Ah Lee,

43

through it all, if it is possible for a Chinaman to add to a profound natural reserve, he did so.

The other shade of the happening that hung over the ship was that the Chinaman had given his devotion whole-heartedly to the second mate, who had taken his part. It seemed that his almost unassailable Oriental soul had been touched by an act of compassion rendered to him by this being of infinite remoteness — a greater remoteness than that existing between an officer of a ship and a Chinese seaman is hard to imagine. While he disregarded, or so it appeared, the very existence of Singleton, his gaze was seldom off Macklin when the latter was about. One might have thought that he feared the second mate was in imminent danger — that something was about to happen to him.

A bright, sunny morning found us docked in Sydney, at the company's wharf, well up the long, deeply indented harbour. Now, although in no wise a man of recognised habits, Singleton had one which he regularly humoured. This was that for the first few minutes of a morning in port he would take up his station on the forward deck next the wharf, where a convenient bollard afforded a footrest. We used to think that his foot must have worn a groove in that particular bollard. He would lean indolently on the rail, with an eye to the opening operations of the ship's derricks as they lifted the cargo out of the hold. Often he would turn and stare downwards at the wharf, as though he were studying it. He was always at the same spot; he came to be looked upon as a fixture there.

The cargo would be swung, sometimes in nets, right over him, so that anyone standing directly underneath could frequently see his head intervening below the burden of the derrick just when this had attained its highest point, stopping with a jerk preparatory to being swung outwards.

The Captain had remarked it at Suva, some days after Singleton had made the kitten a victim of his unprovoked wrath. He suggested to Singleton that he move aside. "Better step aside, there, Mr. Singleton," he had offered in his even manner. "Can't trust too much in these nets. Never can tell. Better be on the safe side."

Singleton had laughed and stayed there longer than was his wont. It was just then that I noticed Ah Lee, who was crossing the deck on some dim mission. At the skipper's words he stopped suddenly and gazed intently, deeply, concentrating, so it seemed, his whole presence on Singleton. Only for a second, naturally; but his demeanour reminded

44

me of a man who had discovered something he was seeking.

This first morning in Sydney found the mate in his customary place, with his arms folded on the rail, staring at the black wharf below as though he were absorbed by it. He was hatless, and his dark hair dully reflected the rays of the sun.

The first net, bulging with crates, lifted slowly up out of the hold and for a moment was there above his head, poised. A ferry was in midstream, I remember, crowded with people going into the city offices.

There was an abrupt sundering noise, a crash, and white crates came tumbling on to the deck and the wharf. They smashed open, scattering the parts of innocent-looking sewing machines that women were to use in the quiet of their rooms. It was all totally without warning, and burst into the precise business of that ship with the fury of an avalanche tearing through the shadowed forests of an unexpectant mountain valley. It came like a thunderclap in a clear sky, and was followed by a grim stillness in which men held their breaths.

I glanced up — I was on the wharf — to where I had last perceived the head of Singleton glinting in the sun. It was not there. He had been hit by one of the falling crates. Instead was a grisly blur of redness against the whiteness of the upper works to whose final white-washing Macklin had seen before we made port. It resembled a splash of red ink suspended in midair, and under it his arms were still folded, his body bent forward, nodding, slightly swaying, as in an attitude of contemplation — of appalled contemplation, as though in one awful instant had been opened to him the closed book of the Inscrutable, as though he had grasped the entire futility of being, had seen the mists rolled back from a future dark and pregnant with unmentionable horror. There was an expression to that fearful trunk that a second before had breathed life.

Then it toppled back onto the deck, as if a hand had plucked it from behind, importuned it away from its ghastly cogitation. It fell with a thud sounding loud in the silence that pervaded that ship.

The derrick's net was lowered, for no reason. A man covered with grime ran forward, picked it up, looked at it. "Cut — ropes cut!" he shouted, as though that could alter things. No one paid any attention to him. He retreated quickly to save himself from an overwhelming dismay.

That is all I know, except that as I reached the deck Macklin strode forward from nowhere, apparently, with incomprehension on his face,

45

and that Ah Lee, a figure of grey, coming silently on the scene, as silently as a shadow glanced first at Macklin, then at Singleton's body. Before it had been taken to the cabin the Chinaman had walked off the ship.

Now, whether one dark night Ah Lee had gained access to the locker and cut through the ropes of the nets — for we found them all similarly affected — until they barely held, hoping that in some inexplicable fashion they would not sunder until their burden was over the mate's head — Singleton's head — and then, by the intervention of his Chinese gods, come apart; whether his heart had engendered that extent of hatred against Singleton; and whether at the last he had been aghast at the success of his plan and fled for ever from its locality I do not know, although I have heard Captain Burrows advance just those views.

I only know that I, or any other member of that ship's company, have not seen Ah Lee since. He vanished utterly, as shadows do, into the dust that hangs about unkept corners of a city cosmopolitan in its nature.

# Slim from the Chilcotin

HOWARD O'HAGAN

*A version of this story, "The Man Who Took Chilcotin to Australia," was published in the Victoria* Colonist, *13 January 1963. The manuscript version is held by the University of Victoria.*

Slim Conway — it is not his real name — was a cow-hand from the Chilcotin in the Cariboo — and looked the part. He was dark, tall and lean, wore high-heeled riding-gaiters, a blue serge suit, a purple neckerchief and a black Stetson hat. The lid of his left eye drooped, but the other eye, from under the rolled-up brim of his hat, stared out steady and unblinking, like an eye along a rifle barrel.

I met him in a strange environment: third-class on the old R.M.S. *Aorangi*, going down to Sydney, N.S.W., from Vancouver many years ago. I had just finished a season as a guide up at Jasper, Alberta, and with some money in my pocket had set out to "see the world." Slim was on a similar mission, having been left a few hundred pounds by the death of an uncle in England.

Slim, of course, had never been in England. A young man in his twenties, his travels, until he boarded the *Aorangi* for "down under" that December so long ago, had been limited to winter trips from the ranch in the Chilcotin to Vancouver.

I first spoke to him a day or so before Christmas when we were not far out of Suva in the Fijis. He was standing by the rail, up towards the bow of the ship, the ends of his purple neckerchief blown against his shoulder, his thin beak of a nose splitting the wind. Great blue rollers, uneasy hills of water, moved towards us, lifting the vessel up and slowly letting it fall. Slim and I gazed out from the rail, both of us, I think,

47

appalled at the vast expanse of the Pacific Ocean.

We found a common interest in horses and when we reached Sydney ten days later, put up at the same hotel. Despite my urging, Slim would not change his clothes for more conventional attire and during the weeks that followed, the high-crowned hat, the flowing neckerchief, the high-heeled gaiters drew a good deal of attention along the streets of downtown Sydney. And not much of it was friendly. Australians seemed to take these manly, but alien, accoutrements as an affront to their national pride. Slim's attitude was that "what's good enough up home, is good enough down here."

Trouble was brewing. It was only a matter of time. It came one late afternoon in a bar on lower George Street down near the Circular Quay where, in those days, the ferry-boats docked. Over his third whiskey, Slim let out a wild, high-pitched cowboy shriek. After its echoes died away, a silence settled on the bar, almost as palpable as falling snow. It was broken when a short, stocky individual on my left, turned and hit me on the nose. Why he chose me as his victim, rather than Slim, I do not know. I guess it was enough that we were both Canadians and each responsible for the other.

When the dust had settled, Slim and I were out beyond the swinging doors, picking ourselves up from the pavement. We were slightly battered. One of Slim's eyes was closing. I had a cut lip and my cheek was bleeding. We went home to Mrs. Donovan's on King's Cross above Woolloomooloo to nurse our wounds — for, by this time, our funds dwindling, we had left the hotel for a rooming-house.

Both Slim and I wanted to get a job on a sheep or cattle station out in the "back-blocks." These outfits — the large ones — had offices in Sydney but when we applied there we were told to come back when we had had some "Australian experience." The mystery of how we would acquire that experience, when we were given no chance to show what we could do, was never explained to us.

By April we were "on the beach" and sleeping out in the "Domain," a park-like place off Boomerang Street between the centre of town and Woolloomooloo, a tough working-class district where, after sun-down, a man walked in the middle of the street, away from lanes and shadows. The summer heat was now over and the nights were chill. We slept under newspapers, preferably the want-ad sections after having read them. The want-ad pages, Slim said, were warmer. The head-lines of the other sections "let in the air."

48

He still adhered to his original preference in the way of clothes, though the blue suit was far past its prime and the heels of the riding-gaiters badly worn down. After a few days and nights of the Domain, I got a job as a day-labourer and later sold real-estate. Slim and I drifted apart.

I saw him once more, a few days before I shipped out for Montreal as an ordinary seaman — the most "ordinary" seaman that the Swedish first-mate of the *Canadian Scottish* had ever come up against. This day I noticed Slim because of his high hat. It was in the evening on the corner of Pitt and King streets, then a district of theatres and restaurants. Down Pitt Street towards the water-front was the main post office, on Phillip's Square. The front of the post-office was composed of a series of arcades and stone columns. Here, towards dark, waiting for the men coming up from the water-front after their day's work, women would gather to the number of two or three score. Once in a while detectives would descend upon them and chase them out of the shadows into the lights of Pitt Street and up Pitt to King.

It was in one of these enforced migrations that Slim had somehow been caught. With others I stood back as the screaming, many-skirted procession passed by. Carried along in its midst, his black hat over-topping the women's heads, was Slim, incongruous as an antlered moose would be entangled in a herd of domestic stock. I called out to him. He did not hear. I tried to get to him. The press of the crowd was too great.

In later years I have lived on Howe Sound and watched the Union Steamship ferries going up to Squamish to connect with the Pacific Great Eastern to the Cariboo and often wondered if among their passengers I might one day meet my friend Slim of the Chilcotin. I believe he loved his native hills too well to long forsake them for a distant land. After all, he took all of the Chilcotin with him that he could when he sailed away for Australia. He wore its clothes and one day surely he would bring them back.

49

# Accepted by the Penguins

### HOWARD O'HAGAN

*The manuscript of this story is held
by the University of Victoria.*

Standing in the dock in the harbor of Montevideo, Uruguay, that sunny spring morning in the mid-30s, was a tall white ship. She was the R.M.S. *Reina del Pacifico*, 17,000 tons. She was out of Southampton, England, on a cruise around South America. I had come over to her the previous night by boat across the River Plate from Buenos Aires in the Argentine.

I had been there, in Buenos Aires, for two years as *Jefe de Publicidad* — "Chief of Publicity" — in a British-owned railway, running north to semi-tropical Tucuman and north-west to the Sierra de Cordoba. Except for these "hills of Cordoba" in its geographical centre, and the Andes in the far west, the Argentine is very flat country, indeed. Compared to its pampas, the Canadian prairies are a succession of hills and dales.

A man raised in the mountains becomes lonely for them. Therefore, when I read in the papers that the *Reina del Pacifico* would be touching at Montevideo and from there proceeding to the Falkland Islands, through the Magellan Straits and up the southern and mountainous coast of Chile to Puerto Montt, I decided to take three weeks leave of my job and go that far with her. From Puerto Montt I would cross east over the Andes by horse and launch on the several lakes, to the rail-head at Bariloche and from there by train across Patagonia to Buenos Aires.

I had another reason for my journey: on the British-owned railway I suffered from two distinctions. Among its thirty-thousand odd Argentine Spanish-speaking employees and its four hundred, equally odd, English-born executives, I was the only Canadian. I was also the

50

youngest by many years to attend the monthly meetings of its Chief Officers. It seemed to me that the time had come to abjure for a while these two onerous disabilities.

On boarding the *Reina del Pacifico* and setting out into the South Atlantic, neither my comparative youth — I was thirty-one — nor my Canadian origins could be held against me. Many younger people were aboard and, as for my being Canadian, no one outside the stewards and the man on my left at table, knew about it until we had left the Falkland Islands for the good reason that, until then, no one else had spoken to me. My presence aroused quite a different prejudice. It was some time before I discovered what it was.

The passenger-list was made up almost exclusively of people from the British Isles. We had among us one Baronet, three "Sirs," two with "Hon." before their names and their ladies. Besides these were an Italian family and two Germans who had come aboard, as I later learned, at Rio de Janeiro. The two Germans were the first Nazis I had met.

And there was one other who with me had joined the ship at Montevideo. Tall, black-bearded, wearing a black cloak and black, wide-brimmed black hat, he might have been a character out of W.H. Hudson's *Far Away and Long Ago*. On board ship it is usual to walk the deck counter-clock wise. The man in black on his pre-prandial strolls, consistently walked in the reverse direction, solitary, aloof, against the human stream which parted to make way for him. Nor did he dress for dinner.

The first morning out of Montevideo, in flannels and rubber-soled shoes, I went hopefully up to the top deck for a game of deck-tennis. There were two courts on which the players, while I stood there, several times, having finished their games, gave up their places to others. No one invited me to play.

Before lunch at the bar I had my drink alone. At lunch, at my table of six, all of them men, the conversation left me out. At the end of the meal, the man on my left asked would I "mind" if he smoked. I told him to go right ahead.

After forty-eight hours we anchored in Port Stanley in the Falklands. There launches took us ashore and we set out over-land on a three-mile hike "to see the penguins." The part of the Falklands which I saw that day was undulating untimbered country, much like the Rockies above tree-line. It is good country for raising sheep.

Only about two hundred of the ship's passengers made the hike across the hills, among them the man in the flowing black cloak. I was by myself and was first to reach the penguins.

As I remember them today they were King penguins, more than knee-high. A thousand of them, in their snow jackets, were crowded on the pebbly beach. Facing my approach, they stood unmoving, except for their heads. These turned, the one to the other, as though they were in silent conference which they would, under no circumstances, permit me to interrupt. The stench of fish on which they fed was strong as was the sense of dignity they imparted.

Soon my companions from aboard came over and down the rise to the beach, their many-coloured scarves blowing in the wind, like an army with banners. They swept on down as if they would drive the penguins, and me with them, into the sea. The penguins held their ground, nor did they make a bow. Vaguely I felt that, though denied by the ship's company, I had been accepted by the penguins. Back aboard, the next morning, half an hour before lunch, one of the two "honourables" — today he is high in the British motor industry — met the man in the black cloak directly in front of my chair. As usual, "black-beard" was on his contrary course so that the two almost collided. As they drew back, the other said to "black-beard," "I understand Mr. Ormsby that, at one time, you raised sheep on the Falklands. I would very much like to hear about it."

Ormsby drew himself up to his full and imposing height. "Sir," he said, "twice passing you on deck, have I said 'good morning.' Twice, you have ignored me. Now you can go to Hell."

Late that afternoon, Ormsby came in and sat beside me at the bar. After ordering his whiskey, he turned to me and said, "You heard our conversation this morning in front of your chair?"

I replied that I couldn't help but over-hear it.

"Of course," he went on, "he has my name from the passenger-list, but what I can't make out is how he knew I had been a sheep-rancher on the Falklands." Ormsby had left the Falklands a few years before for Uruguay. He was now a man in his fifties, going back to his home in the north of England.

He said, "You got on at Montevideo, as I did?"

I told him that I had come across from Buenos Aires.

He asked me if I had felt "a bit out of it" on board. I said I had.

"That's the reason," he said. "Most of them on the ship have us tagged as 'natives.' To them we're 'South Americans' and 'out-siders.' A cruise-ship like this becomes a pretty closely knit company after a few weeks together. In a way we're crashing their party."

The catch in this was that Ormsby looked and courted the part ascribed to him. I had no beard. My garb was conventional.

However that may be, before we had passed through the Straits of Magellan, I had had my games of deck-tennis and no longer took my drinks alone. It had required a little time to pass into the ship's social circle.

I left the *Reina del Pacifico* at Puerto Montt, having seen the splendid coastal mountains I set out to see. The two Nazis left with me and we crossed Chile and the Argentine together. I returned to Buenos Aires, still a Canadian and, unfortunately, only three weeks older.

# The Berkeley Arts Club:
# Chronicles by and of
# Howard O'Hagan

E.W. STRONG

The Berkeley Arts Club at the University of California, Berkeley, held its first meeting in April of 1935 with twenty charter members; two of these were not members of the university faculty.[1] Howard O'Hagan became the twenty-fourth member (and the third nonfaculty member) by election at the club meeting that was held on 4 March 1938. He was sponsored by Professor Gordon McKenzie, Department of English. The Club's secretary (the only fixed officer) lists Howard as a reporter and short-story writer.

Ordinarily, during an academic year, the club meetings were held on the first Friday of the month, four times in the fall semester and four in the spring. Beginning in November 1937, the recording of the minutes of club meetings ceased to be the responsibility of the secretary. A substitute was adopted for the minutes, and was given the name "chronicle." Each meeting began with a cocktail party at the home of the host for that meeting. The host was responsible for notifying the membership of place and time of cocktail party and of dinner (usually held at the Faculty Club). Selecting the menu and dinner wine and presiding over the meeting completed the host's duties. Howard served as host at three meetings: 6 December 1940, at Spenger's seafood restaurant in Berkeley; 4 February 1944, at the Faculty Club; 7 December 1945, at the Faculty Club. I was the chronicler of the first of these three meetings. In my chronicle, I note that in his paper "Caricature: Daumier and Dickens," Gordon McKenzie dwells on the tension created by various kinds of conflict in the works of the artist and the novelist. Howard breaks into a quarrel with Gordon, his good friend: "Howard O'Hagan, however, divines a further reach of romanticism, that of conflict within conflict to enhance aesthetic value. Fastening on this truly Irish intuition, he proceeds to test it empirically." His interruption is shushed and rebuked by several members:

> Howard leaves the room to find a more receptive audience for his experiment. Gordon concludes with a discourse on satire as a mixture of serious and comic elements and the discussion had hardly begun when Howard returns from his foray. He had found an audience but had not been able to demonstrate his hypothesis successfully.

Howard had gone to the bar of the restaurant, had there been combative, had been hit, and returned bloodied, protesting bitterly: "the son of a bitch knew I was drunk, but the son of a bitch hit me; the son of a bitch knew I was drunk, but the son of a bitch hit me."

Howard served as the chronicler at four meetings. A chronicler was free to report a meeting in any way he chose. He might indeed write a *chronicle*, in the strict sense of the word: a historical account of facts or events recorded in the order in which they happened. Quite a number of chronicles preserve some fidelity to fact; but quite a few are marked by poetic license. Heights of invention are attained in Howard's three preserved chronicles. (One has disappeared.)

The secretary's records show that Howard read his short stories at the meetings of 14 October 1939 (no records remain), 5 May 1944 (excerpts from the chronicle of this meeting are reprinted here); 1 February 1946 (relevant excerpts by the chronicler, Everett Glass, are reprinted here).

Attendance records were not kept by the secretary, but he did list the host, the reader, and the chronicler for each meeting. Participation of a member in discussion, song, or other proceeding or event may or may not be noted by the chronicler. It is not safe to conclude from an examination of the chronicles how frequently Howard came to meetings, and to what extent he took part in debate. A glance through a sample selection of chronicles indicates that not much of consequence is discoverable. I did find one revealing entry, however. James Caldwell, professor of English, on 3 December 1943, read a paper on Keats in which he devoted most of his attention to the poet's method of composition. A vigorous debate about method ensued. Howard remarked: "The essential thing is *what* he wrote, not *how* he wrote it." The chronicler (Charles Cushing, Department of Music) adds a parenthetical comment: "This was delivered for all the world like Big Business, cutting the throat of a competitor."

## CHRONICLE I

¶ *Chronicle 1 was read at the meeting of 2 October 1942, and is Howard's account of the 2 September meeting. Professor James Cline was the host, and Everett Glass read his play* Catherine the Great.

Mr. Cline walked forth and back, wagging his head. "It goes nowhere," he said, "nowhere. It begins and has no end."

"On the contrary," Mr. McKenzie, pacing beside him, answered. "It seems to end right there, in the woods, beyond the window."

Mr. Cline brought himself up abruptly. He came closer to Mr. McKenzie.

"An appearance," he said in a low voice. He glanced about him. There were others in the room. "An appearance," he continued, "and not the reality. It is a road without destination, but one which I suspect . . ."

"Suspect?" asked Mr. McKenzie.

"Suspect is the word. I suspect it has not been built without purpose, in the night, laid across my lawn, to confront me every morning."

"But, Jim, who would do such a thing?"

"The authorities," Mr. Cline said.

"You mean? . . ." Mr. McKenzie's shoulders were broad. He shrugged them.

"That's what I mean exactly," Mr. Cline said.

At that moment a manacled duck waddled out on to the lawn, paused, stepped upon the road.

"Ducks?" Mr. McKenzie inquired.

"One duck," Mr. Cline said.

"Oh, a clucking duck."

Mr. Cline explained that it was only a mallard. "The beginning," he added, "you might say that I am only at the beginning . . . but now you understand . . . I mean about the road. Of course when the moon comes up over the hills and there is a fog and you cannot see it . . . then the whole scheme becomes apparent."

Mr. Cline looked out at the duck, hesitated. "You see," he said, "the duck cannot fly. He is manacled."

Mr. McKenzie said, "Ah!"

Then he asked, "male or female?"

"Gordon," Mr. Cline said softly, "my relations with my duck are purely formal."

Out of the stillness from behind him, Mr. McKenzie heard Mr. Pepper speak. He had lately returned from New York. He said, "One difference between New York and Berkeley is that, in New York, if you have made a fool of yourself, you merely have to walk to the other side of the block. Or so, at least, I have been told."

Someone called that night was falling. Another enquired "where?" and if anything could be done about it. Then the group of men, nocturnal in habit, peripatetic in thought, arose, left the room, gathered their hats, paid their respects, drove away in their cars. The cars circled Mr. Cline's house, went up the road across its lawn. By the side of the road the duck was nesting.

Mr. McKenzie, passing, raised his brow, nodded, as if to himself.

The road across the lawn led inevitably to a state of mind. On arrival Mr. Cline said, "I would never have believed it. Never — unless I had been told."

There, during dinner, Mr. Löwenberg gave back to Mr. Pepper the leadership of the club. Mr. Pepper reported that in New York he had discovered the record of a club similar to the Arts Club, but unlike it in that all the members smoked pipes.

Later Mr. Benner put the minutes of the last meeting into music, after Mr. Elkus had put music into the piano.

Mr. Everett Glass read a play. It was a play to be called by Mr. Hayes "a morality play set against the background of war."

Mr. Cline and Mr. Löwenberg agreed with Mr. Hayes' definition of the play, Mr. Cline adding that it was to him the story of Everyman.

Mr. Strong and Mr. McKenzie on the other hand emphasized the technique employed — namely one of setting up a background, that of the world we live in today, alive and real to us, in whose awful shadow the dramatic action took place.

The dinner came to a close when Mr. Cline, the host, in his seat by an open window, stirred, became uneasy, at the beat of wings in the night, wild duck winging northward underneath an old, old moon.

## CHRONICLE 2

¶ *Chronicle 2 is divided into two parts. The whole was presented at the meeting of 5 November 1943. Howard is the chronicler, and is recording the 1 October meeting. Howard Moise read a paper entitled "A Site Protested" (the site being that of the Lawrence Radiation Laboratory, which overlooks the Berkeley campus). Mr. Weatherweary and Mr. Blizzard are fictional. The Hotel Whitecotton, Mr. Perry (dean of the School of Architecture), and playwright Mathurin Dondo, are not. In part 1, Howard did not attempt to depict the kind of discourse heard from members of the club, especially the philosophers, on matters aesthetic. The second part of the second chronicle beautifully recalls the substance and essence of Arts Club conversations not captured in the first part. With fidelity and satiric intent, Howard in these pages presents what he heard anent aesthetic experiences, values, and judgements. Who were the discoursers? I recognize Stephen Pepper, Jack Löwenberg, and myself.*

### Part 1

Mr. Weatherweary and Mr. Blizzard reached Berkeley, a west coast town, on the first Friday in October. They had travelled together, Mr. Weatherweary coming directly from the south, and Mr. Blizzard deviously and at great personal danger from the north. They met in Mr. Blizzard's room in the Whitecotton Hotel.

When Mr. Weatherweary entered the room, his friend was pacing the floor. "You see how it is, Samuel," Mr. Blizzard said to him. "You see how it is." He pointed to the window. "The sun is shining. I don't dare leave the premises. Sometimes it is just possible if there is a wind, but in this cursed California climate, there will be no wind. On the whole, Samuel, and by and large, the experiment was not worth the risk."

"There may be wind later when the sun has gone," Mr. Weatherweary said. He was worried, not only by the attitude, but also by the appearance of his friend, Blizzard. Blizzard, usually only a wailing ghost of a figure, now was robust, firm of step, decided in his manner.

"I tell you what, Daniel," he said to Mr. Blizzard. "I will go out and walk the streets and enquire if, after the sun has set, there will be wind."

"By all means, Samuel, and at once."

So Mr. Weatherweary went out and walked the streets to enquire for wind. In the north end of the town, he met a man who was urging what seemed to be a piece of grey radiator down a hill. The man paused and asked Mr. Weatherweary to accompany him. After he had seated himself, the man behind the wheel said to him, "It's like this. You merely get behind this wheel and push and it goes. Marvellous, no one knows why, but it does."

Mr. Weatherweary remarked that it did, and was about to make a further observation when he noticed that the man at whose side he sat was one whose brow, for his wisdom, had been enlarged by God. Mr. Weatherweary was silent.

"We are going," said the strange driver, "to the house of a man who keeps ducks. That is to say, he wishes to keep ducks. He has the facilities, but, the landlord objects. However, he does keep ducks. No one knows of it. It is a secret between him and the landlord."

Mr. Weatherweary was taken to the home of the man who kept ducks. Other men were there. Each had his own name. One stood by the fire-place and rubbed his nose. Another closer to the door had his hand in his trouser pocket. Others were there also. They drank and ate. Once Mr. Weatherweary thought he heard the hum of wind in the chimney, but he could not be sure.

While he attended he felt near to him the shadow, the breath, the form, the substance of beauty and he was content. Still he was not permitted to stay and was carried away in another direction entirely.

"We are now on our way to dinner," the owner of the grey radiator said to him.

"To dinner."

"Yes, at the club."

Mr. Weatherweary asked which club it was.

"It is the Faculty Club at the University."

"Oh, the university."

His companion regarded him closely. "I said the University," he said. "You will see when you get there. It is an uneasy state of mind surrounded by professors."

After dinner one of the men, although threatened by those around him, read a paper. He was a Mr. Moise. He pointed out that an untoward activity was taking place on the hills above the university campus. Trees were being scattered and grass uprooted. And what, he demanded, was the end of this activity? It was that some members of the staff, having found an atom, were interested in housing it so that they might afterwards tear it to pieces, bit by bit.

That in itself, said Mr. Moise, was bad enough, but he would not stand out against it. We all have our failings. What he did object to was the method. This atom was to be set loose under a series of Renaissance arches and run to earth. Atoms, asserted Mr. Moise, suffer to the supportable limit under arches of any sort. Give an atom a chance and it will run a mile from a Renaissance arch. But this atom would only be able to run from one Renaissance arch to another. There was every probability that in its extremity the atom, shattered by the illogic of its experiences, would escape from between the arches. Mr. Moise did not desire to contemplate the consequences of a shattered atom loose upon the campus, much less within the class-rooms. Professors, he implied but did not state, have already as much as they can bear. Steps should be taken to assure that the atom would have that sort of shelter to which it was accustomed, and for which it would have a natural affinity. Mr. Moise showed some moving pictures of what an atom might be expected to require in this respect.

Further to the point Mr. Moise read an article written by another Mr. Moise in the *Harvard Advocate* which showed how a university president, confronted by a countess with fifty million franks in her reticule, was unable to do what the lady wished. But he was an eastern university president and was going to try God-damned hard. The members at dinner thought this a good idea and applauded.

Then a Mr. Perry, on Mr. Weatherweary's left, rose up to speak. He said he did not feel that controversial subjects should be brought before the meetings. Mr. Macpherson, a tall, lean man, with determined shoulders, who was not present, replied that inasmuch as the proposal made by Mr. Perry was itself controversial he did not see how it could be discussed without violating what he took to be the intention of its sponsor.

There was a commotion and an uprising on Mr. Weatherweary's right. A voice, at first low and then loud, said "And the Lord said, 'Let them have it.' "

A Mr. Pepper, with whom Mr. Weatherweary was surprised to see that he had come to the dinner, stated that he saw no reason why the Arts Club — he explained for Mr. Weatherweary's benefit that he was now attending a meeting of the Arts Club — should not bring to the attention of the authorities what was happening when it did and if it did.

Mr. Moise said any modern building was convertible.

A Mr. Löwenberg said he was a philosopher and that the public owned public buildings. A man might avoid a symphony because he had to have tickets to go to it. He would not avoid a public building unless he went into it.

A Mr. Strong said he was also a philosopher and the thing to do was to treat all questions of function in logical form. There should be a connection between those controlling the form and those concerned in its function.

A Mr. Dondo wished to know if questions were controversial because they were vital. A work of art is a whole and not a chapter. His opinion was that the atom might be housed in the Pantheon in Rome.

Mr. Macpherson who was still present made several final asseverations, one of them immediately over the head of Mr. Weatherweary.

Returning to the Whitecotton Hotel early in the morning, Mr. Weatherweary reassured Mr. Blizzard, "It is quite all right, Daniel," he said. "You may go abroad. Though there is no wind, except in certain places, and though the sun shines, you will not be in any way conspicuous."

### Part 2

Mr. Weatherweary, a long harried man, paced back and forth in his room on the second storey of the Hotel Whitecotton. His friend and travelling companion, Mr. Blizzard, from a chair by the cold fire-place watched him, not narrowly, but with eyes wide-open.

Mr. Blizzard was on his guard. Since becoming an honorary member of the Arts Club, Mr. Weatherweary had been given to queer, sudden movements. Especially on a night of rain such as this when he had returned from a meeting, he was apt, with no warning at all, to dodge behind a chair, shift a picture from its proper place upon the wall, rattle the knob of the door or go to the window, open it and shout "Thalatta! Thalatta!," believing that he was the subject or the object of aesthetic contemplation on a hill top alone and that below him was the sea.

Mr. Blizzard, a man of experience, took it calmly, assuming that his friend merely modelled his behaviour upon that of those with whom he had passed the evening. Nevertheless, he was on his guard.

"Well," he said at last as Mr. Weatherweary paused in indecision beside the window.

Mr. Weatherweary turned. His eyes had attained a certain hunted look.

"A tall man," he said, "dark. Quite dark and very tall."

"Nothing remarkable in that," Mr. Blizzard replied. "I remember, indeed, in Persia and in parts of Northwestern Asia . . ."

"A tall dark man," Mr. Weatherweary continued, "and he spoke . . ."

Mr. Blizzard removed the pipe from his mouth. A tall dark man who spoke. . . . This was . . . that is to say if he spoke there would undoubtedly be implications.

"You mean there were implications?" he asked.

Mr. Weatherweary nodded.

"But first of all he said, "there was this house, surrounded by trees. A road — unmistakably a road — went up to it, avoiding the trees. The road led to the door. I mean by that not quite to the door, but to the steps before the door. Still there was no going back, having gone that far. I entered through the door. Others, however, I observed coming in through the window, quietly, in ones and twos, alone and with one another. These men stood about holding glasses. It was what might be called a group gathering, or, if you prefer the term, collective drinking. That is to say, though each drank separately, they drank together, a notable performance of its sort."

Mr. Weatherweary approached Mr. Blizzard's chair. He leaned over, whispered. "I learned on leaving," he added, "that it was the house of a Mr. Benner, and the dark man was there among them, the one who was to speak."

Mr. Blizzard rubbed his ear, his own ear.

Mr. Weatherweary resumed his march across the room. Over his shoulder he called out, "Then in motor cars we went to the university, a place of green lawns, frolic and laughter where a brook runs and in the shadows wisdom lingers. There, in a club, across a tabled vineyard, the man who was dark, found his words and spoke."

"His name?" asked Mr. Blizzard.

"He spoke, that was sufficient," said Mr. Weatherweary, coming close to the fireplace. Before his friend could interfere, he dropped to his knees, crawled into it, struggled until he had wedged his shoulders firmly in the chimney. Then in a voice, still his voice, but yet another heavy, portentous voice issued from it to the room: "Strikingly different" it intoned, "as these three types of judgment are, they are frequently confused and sometimes telescoped into one." (Here it was evident that Mr. Weatherweary . . . [the remainder of this sentence was inserted in pencil, and defies my attempts to decipher it!].) "And as regards the first two, at least, there is no general agreement as to which should be given dominance or priority over the other."

Mr. Blizzard rose, walked to the window, stood there, hands clasped behind his back, staring out to the rain polished street. The voice from the chimney went on, continued, grew in volume, had its way. "But to attribute aesthetic value to a work of art," it said, "is an error, except in a manner of speaking. As a stimulus it is a cause of aesthetic values, but these values are solely those of pleasant experiences actually had. . . . A critic writing about a work of art is either simply reporting his experiences in its presence or predicting other people's probable experiences in its presence. On the basis of these predictions, it may well acquire so-called commercial value."

The voice boomed. It shook the hotel to its foundations. In the lobby bells rang. Doors opened and shut. In the corridor, people murmured, talked, called loudly. Mr. Blizzard ran to the wall, pushed his own bell.

After a while an attendant came. Mr. Blizzard gave his order.

While he waited, Mr. Weatherweary's feet disappeared up the chimney, the voice rose higher and higher. "Immediate experience," were the words that came to Mr. Blizzard as the attendant entered with logs, moss, a green branch of Douglas fir, and kindling.

"Right there," Mr. Blizzard said, "well back against the wall."

When the attendant had gone and the flame in the fireplace was sputtering, he sat in the chair, lit his pipe. In such cases he knew there was only one remedy, only one thing to do: to enjoy your pipe. Take your time and smoke him out.


### CHRONICLE 3

¶ *Chronicle 3 was presented by Howard at the meeting of 2 May 1947, and is his account of the meeting held on 11 April, at which Donald McLaughlin acted as host, and Professor Albert Elkus, chairman of the Music Department, exhibited and illustrated a musical composition at the piano. (I seem to remember that it was a Beethoven sonata.) Howard begins by noting a lapse of many years since Mr. Weatherweary last attended a meeting of the Arts Club. Hardith and Meredy, reported to be "standing by the fire-place," are the speakers in the dialogues written by Professor Löwenberg (of the Department of Philosophy) for the Arts Club, and collected in* Dialogues from Delphi *(published by the University of California Press in 1949). Mr. Weatherweary sees "Brother O'Hagan, one of the lesser but more conscientious members of the fraternity, busily taking notes."*

It was a long time, years ago, indeed, since Mr. Weatherweary had attended a meeting of the Arts Club of which he was an honorary member. Now, as on that former occasion, he was unable to bring with him his friend and travelling companion, Mr. Blizzard. Mr. Blizzard was resting as comfortably as could be expected in his room at the Whitecotton Hotel, recovering from a bout with the west wind.

Mr. Weatherweary became a trifle worried as he walked along the street beneath the blossoms towards Donald McLaughlin's house. He was perturbed because on his first and only previous appearance at the Arts Club, when his touch was surer, his eye less clouded, his step more spry, he had described the place where many of the members passed their time, that is to say, the university, as "an uneasy state of mind surrounded by professors." On this second Friday in April of 1947 he feared that the remark might be held against him.

He need not have worried. He was admitted to the house, given a glass to hold and not otherwise regarded. Peeping out from his corner, for he was by nature a retiring man, Mr. Weatherweary looked about for changes that the years had brought. Here, too, he found cause for reassurance. The same voices, the same words, the same emphases and the same subtleties were around him. As before, there were big dogs and little dogs and each dog, in his own fashion, one with a rumbling roar, another shrilly, barked as well as he could. Being a student of Chekhov, Mr. Weatherweary knew that this was as it should be.

One minor change he noticed. Hardith and Meredy were standing by the fire-place, still drinking from their unfathomable cup. But, whereas before, each had sipped in turn, handing the cups forth and back with commendable politeness, and sometimes with dignity, this afternoon they were taking huge and simultaneous draughts from their common receptacle. The achievement filled Mr. Weatherweary with awe.

Seeing Brother O'Hagan, one of the lesser but more conscientious members of the fraternity, busily taking notes, — a duty to which, it was to be supposed, he had submitted in his usual fashion of agreement without conditions as to the subject of his chronicle, — seeing this diligent and persevering man trying to extract, order and perhaps even reason from the chaos of his surroundings, Mr. Weatherweary recalled that the occasion was to be more than one of audacious tail wagging and haphazard barks. That is to say, that there was a man chosen for the occasion. To put it briefly, some one, come Hell or high-water, was to read a paper — but not, of course, until his hearers had so befuddled themselves with wine and drowsed themselves with food as to be unable to understand what he said.

Mr. Weatherweary cast about to see who this happy man might be. After a few moments he told himself no mistake was possible. There could be no mistaking the crimson tie, the calm certainty of posture, the outthrust chest, nor yet the glazed and defiant eye of Albert Elkus. He was the evening's chosen victim and, by God, his attitude suggested, he would make the others suffer with him! If it was music they wanted, he would give it to them — in words. He would use the piano only as a prop.

And, as Mr. Weatherweary discovered when the group had adjourned to the Faculty Club for dinner, there was no piano in the room, not even under the table, for he left his chair and crawled about to be sure. Returning to his place, he was aware that Albert had come prepared for just this emergency. As Mr. Weatherweary watched, the table rose. It rose slowly but perceptibly until at his eye level it became in a manner not really explicable, attached to Albert's chest. It was now a platform and Albert, while still sitting at it, climbed upon it and began to test the piano which, inevitably, waited for him there. It was a feat not to be lightly brushed aside, even by an architect — and it wasn't, not until another two hours had passed.

It was true that some one had mumbled a word or two about there being a piano in the next room and some of the members may have believed — during those two hours it was possible to believe almost anything — they may have believed that they had left the table and gone in there to listen to Albert. But not Mr. Weatherweary and decidedly not Albert. It would have been impossible, for one thing, for Albert to have pushed that platform through the door.

No, Mr. Weatherweary stayed at the table and Albert stayed on his platform and on his revolving stool. Being a revolving stool it had advantages. Twirling abruptly around from the piano after he had struck a chord — and he was resolute in never striking more than two or three at a time — Albert confronted, he confronted, what else but himself? Then, facing the piano again, he could tap himself on the shoulder and twirl once more. Mr. Weatherweary observed that not once, however though the opportunity was there before him, an opportunity which few men have had, not once did he pat himself upon the back.

Albert touched the piano then twirled and threw words such as "monody" and "fragmentation" into his own face. There were other words, also, many of them, and once in a while a note from the piano. As the minutes progressed, so did Albert. With each half-hour he twirled faster and faster on the stool until his features, his entire body, with the red tie flying from it, became a blur and his other face, above the platform, studying this prodigious progeny, his other self upon the stool, assumed an aspect of mild alarm. As well it might, thought Mr. Weatherweary, a bit alarmed himself.

Then suddenly the scene altered. This was probably at the moment when Albert fell off the stool and the platform collapsed. At any rate, Mr. Weatherweary found himself in the other room with the other members of the club and Albert, undeniably himself, flushed, but not otherwise apparently affected, leaning against the wall. Every one leaned against the wall. Nothing else remained to do.

Mr. Weatherway now paid his hurried respects to the host and the reader and made his way unsteadily to the door. It was high time to go. He had left the window open in the room of the Whitecotton Hotel and for all he knew Mr. Blizzard might have escaped and already be laying the green country-side waste.

### CHRONICLE 4

¶ *Chronicle 4 consists of excerpts from my own record of the 5 May 1944 meeting of the Arts Club, at which Howard O'Hagan read two stories, versions of "The Woman Who Got On at Jasper Station" and "The Tepee."*

The stories themselves were artful in their simplicity. The first concerned the woman who got on at Sacramento, and the second the man who got on in the tepee. The woman got off on the pretext of meeting her husband; the man got off and met the husband. The woman who got on at Sacramento might have been pleased but she was not satisfied. The husband in the second story was satisfied if the man was pleased with his wife. The first story ended, and the second one stopped.

Jim Caldwell opened the discussion with episcopal declarations. The first story was a good story, the second was a bad story. The first story had human significance, a more delicate treatment. The second story was told only in physical terms.

Worth continued the moral censure by coming to the defense of men in the great out-of-doors, Indians or backwoodsmen, declaring that they were not in fact as Howard's fiction had depicted them.

Whereupon Donald [exclaimed], "Woodsman, spare that Cree!"

Further discussion between Gordon and Jim decided that a third man was one too many candidates for initiation into the lodge. Further, it was agreed that not enough was made of the Indian brave's ability to lift a horse. Had this phenomenon been played up in the apprehension of the trapper, the scene between trapper and Indian would have had more suspense.

Donald returned to the moral basis of criticism emphasized by Worth. The affair in the tepee, he said, was not saved from being sordid by the pretext of firewood stacked and unstacked at the entrance. (The way the woodpile was stacked let the returning husband know whether he should enter immediately or wait a while.)

At this point, a transition by way of Montana Pete was made to the first story. Gordon said something about conscious but unspoken mind. Jim wanted more done in the story to reveal habit in the woman since, he thought, habit decided in the end. Both Gordon and Jim agreed on utmost care and delicacy in the treatment of the erotic element in the story. Though no-one had raised the question, Stephen asserted that the erotic theme in the first story was legitimate. Howard O'Hagan was less concerned about that than by what Jim meant by "Utmost care and delicacy."

"Why not a more important theme?" asked Jack, who went on to find the theme not worthy of the talent displayed by the author in his handling of it. Howard Moise disagreed. "The woman," he said, "will regret having missed the opportunity all the rest of her life." Worth disagreed with Howard [Moise] by disparaging the quality of the opportunity and the causal nature of the meeting on the *train*.

# CHRONICLE 5

¶ *Chronicle 5 is Everett Glass's assessment of the short story read by Howard O'Hagan at the Arts Club meeting of 1 February 1946.*

I am not at all sure that I understood the original short story which Howard read. And for that I am truly sorry, because in order to appreciate a work of art properly, I have often heard that we should understand clearly what the artist's intention was in creating it, as well as admit him the privilege of doing it in his own way, from whatever premise he elects. If doing it his own way happens to obscure our understanding of it — that is *our* tough luck, and also the artist's, providing, of course, that our understanding of it is of any importance to him. The theme of Howard's story was simple enough. The soul of a Mr. Wimple, one of our leading advertisers, appears caught between two obsessions, one, the navel of his secretary, Winifred, the other, jealousy of a Mr. Warpington, a rival advertiser. Mr. Wimple is thus a slave of two desires, the one to possess, the other to destroy. These very recognizable and powerful motivations of human behavior give Mr. Wimple whatever semblance of reality he possesses. The other two characters in the story seem to have little reality of their own, being hardly more than sketchy projections of Mr. Wimple's two moods. The plot of the story — if we may define plot somewhat loosely as the things the characters do because the characters are what they are, is likewise uncomplicated as I recall it. Mr. Wimple (whose father, Willy Wimple for no very good reason had been killed by a horse) apparently owns the building in which his advertising firm is located. Mr. Daniel Warpington, the rival advertiser (who for no very good reason wrote poetry when he lived in the East) came West and built a taller building right across the street from Mr. Wimple's. He was evidently successful. And Mr. Wimple, although presumably an American, did not relish so much free competition. In the dark folds of his mind, he spent much time plotting ways of undermining Mr. Warpington. He finally decided upon the unusual — if somewhat costly — method of building the Wimple building several stories down into the ground, while Mr. Warpington's went up into the air. Mr. Wimple had a secretary, Winifred, who was his secret sorrow. Whenever she entered his office, as I have hinted, her navel became the focal point of Mr. Wimple's interest . . . to the obliteration of all else. He was completely absorbed, fascinated by it. When she leaned over his desk, it came dangerously close, yet in a sense it was always far away. By association, it even became confused with the pearl-headed call button on his desk. But for an advertiser, Wimple was very shy. He never told his love. . . . But one day in the interests of better business, he put an ad (with his picture) in an advertising magazine, with a caption "It is later than you think." For some reason (unknown to most brokers on Montgomery St.) this ad created a furor in the stock market. Outside of Mr. W.'s office things rose and fell. Glancing triumphantly out of his window at about this time, to his unspeakable consternation, he saw his rival, Warpington, standing on a window balcony. And beside him stood Winifred, her navel just above the railing. Added to that, at about this same moment, someone brought him a copy of the magazine in which his picture appeared. On the page opposite his picture, Warpington had a huge ad: "It's late in the morning and late in the afternoon," and above the caption, a picture of Winifred in the diaphanous drapes of a reclining model! As if all of this were not enough, a final twist of visceral agony was added. By artful design, or by accident, when the two pages were closed, one over the other, Mr. Wimple's nose fell upon Winifred's navel. But somehow or other, that brought them together again. I don't recall exactly how, but Winifred returned, and — as clearly as I can remember — at the end, Mr. Wimple, though doubled over with his pains of love, looks forward to its inevitable if remote consummation. That, roughly — but not I hope too roughly — is the movement or action of the story. Now of course everyone knows, whether he writes or reads, that listing the characters and outlining the action is not the whole score. How the material is handled, rather than its raw substance makes the difference and the distinction. The plot and characters of Howard's story have little relation, it seems to me, to external reality as most of us know it. He calls Wimple an advertising man, but he might as well be a shoe merchant. As I get it, what Howard is concerned with is the analysis and projection of Wimple's two obsessions. Those two interwoven moods come across to me clearly and insistently, by the sheer concentration of the writing — its sustained tension — terse economy — acrid humor — and occasional sardonic image — such as the rutting buffalo in a dress suit. If the author's intention was to make me dislike Wimple without pitying him, he succeeded. He also made me admire the craftsmanship with which the story was told. Beyond that, I admit, I do not know what his intention may have been. As to whether the story falls into the classic or romantic category, since we now know that those terms have no actuality in themselves, I would play safe and say it did both. Others, liking to appear more modern, might say that it flirts with the subconscious, sur-realism, and borders on what may possibly be called the skiz-o-phrenic school. I will leave the final comment to Victor la Grave. He stated what might, I suppose, be called the realistic approach when he said: "It took Mr. Wimple a long time to get to it. I'd have had the temperature of that navel in about two days."

[1] The chronicles upon which this article is based are now held by the University of California, Berkeley (see, in this volume, Richard Arnold, "Howard O'Hagan: An Annotated Bibliography" A7).

# O'Hagan's Picnic on Cowichan Bay: Memories

E.W. STRONG

I don't think it was mere pleasure in competition. Perhaps it was ancestral. Anyway, Howard O'Hagan welcomed a contest for the sheer joy of being a participant, even though he had little or no chance of emerging victorious. I discovered this soon after he joined the Berkeley Arts Club on 4 March 1938. We members were at Gordon McKenzie's home for cocktails preceding dinner at the Faculty Club. Howard challenged me to arm wrestle with him. Why? I outweighed him by at least 20 pounds, and towered several inches above him. Curiosity induced me to accept. No sooner were our hands locked than Howard bounced up and down and howled like a banshee; he persisted until I ended the unequal match. One would have thought he was in agony. He was enjoying himself. I speak first of this strain in Howard because one needs to know it was there if one is to grasp the fact that what he attempted to do after a picnic he had organized on Cowichan Bay, absurd though it appeared, was not aberrational — it was in character.

When Howard learned in the spring of 1946 that I would be teaching in the summer term at the University of British Columbia in Vancouver, he and Margaret invited me and my family to join them for a weekend. Howard wanted to see Cowichan Lake, and so we went together on the Saturday of my visit. Perhaps the lake has again become a pleasant place to be, but what we gazed upon that day was a body of water surrounded by hillsides cleared of timber. What had been streams were now mere trickles over gravel. Howard said he would take us on a picnic the next morning. We would have lunch on an island in Cowichan Bay.

Howard had one rowboat, and borrowed another from a neighbour. Our family numbered five with our three children: Ann (16), Dick (14), Douglas (10). My wife had asked what we should bring for the picnic lunch, and had been assured that the O'Hagan household and nature

71

were going to take care of us. Before placing an oar in the water, we inspected our boat, and I was prompted to inquire about the distance to be rowed. The fact that we found several inches of water in the boat was not in itself a source of anxiety. Disquiet was, however, fostered by the discovery that continual bailing with a gallon can was needed to stay even with the inflow. The waterlogged boat rowed sluggishly. In my youth, I had rowed with my father on the Willamette River in Oregon (in a two-seater, outrigged), and knew how to handle the oars. That had been a pleasure.

We pulled up on the island on a falling tide. At full ebb, we would harvest seafood from the sands, and then have lunch. But this bounty of nature was not offered. On this day, a phenomenon apparently known to the natives but not, unhappily, anticipated by us, took place before our eyes. Receding only halfway, the tide turned. No clams could be had. Margaret had brought a loaf of bread to eat with the gathered seafood. For dessert, the children found a few wild raspberries.

It was on the return row, when we were some two hundred yards from our home shore, that the absurdity that I mentioned earlier flashed forth. I realized that Howard was trying to engage me in a boat race to the shore! And what was more, I would, by God, have taken him on in complete assurance of defeating him had I been rowing a seaworthy craft and not a tub awash in several inches of seawater.

# Howard O'Hagan, *Tay John*, and the Growth of Story

W.J. KEITH

Howard O'Hagan's importance in Canadian literature — and especially in the literature of western Canada — stems, I believe, from his ability to combine two traditions of narration, the written novel and the oral tale. *Tay John* is itself a novel containing a motley collection of tales, and of tale-tellers. The first part employs omniscient narration and contains both Indian legend and white history, but the second, appropriately entitled "Hearsay," abruptly introduces the reader to Jack Denham, who becomes the narrator of the rest of the book. Denham is a crucial figure, not only because he belongs among the "loners" who, O'Hagan writes in *Wilderness Men*, "are the product of a civilization whose society they have, in large part, rejected" (11), but also because he is an irrepressible collector and teller of tales. Indeed, we first hear of him as one who has returned to Edmonton from the country of the Yellowhead Pass "with a tale" (75) — a tale that, like the Ancient Mariner's, he is impelled to relate to anyone who will listen:

> He would talk about it anywhere — in a pause during dinner at the hotel. He would allude to it suddenly at the bar among strangers over the second glass of whisky. . . . He might meet a friend at the street corner and follow him to his destination, talking, stretching his story the length of Edmonton. It became known as "Jackie's Tale." It was a faith — a gospel to be spread, that tale, and he was its only apostle. Men winked over it, smiled at it, yet listened to its measured voice, attentions caught, imaginations cradled in a web of words. (77)

Denham proceeds to tell the story of his first encounter with Tay John, and then goes on to assemble all the information about the half-breed that he can find, some at first hand but much of it from other sources

73

— a trader, a police inspector, a trapper. This form is not, of course, original. A reader familiar with Conrad's *Lord Jim* will inevitably recall the structure of that novel, in which the distanced third-person narration of the opening gives way to the voice of Marlow (another ancient mariner) and his garrulous, indefatigable probing of the mystery surrounding Jim. Conrad, ex-adventurer and master mariner, provided O'Hagan with an inspiring example in the way he had drawn his material from seamen's yarns and his own experiences in remote places, and then evolved artistic strategies to incorporate this hoard of story into the fabric of the English novel. O'Hagan himself was able to find a means of preserving part of the rich heritage of stories that, through the likes of Jack Denham, represented a strong but essentially oral tradition of tale-telling among the "wilderness men" of the Canadian West. In the process, he learned a great deal about the way that such stories can develop. The unique qualities of his work in general, and of *Tay John* in particular, can best be appreciated when seen in relation to the gradual evolution from oral yarn to written fiction.

This process has been obscured by the accidents of chronology. *Tay John*, although O'Hagan's first book, developed out of his considerable experience of western tale-telling, but his own versions of these tales, to be found in *Wilderness Men* and *The Woman Who Got On at Jasper Station*, did not appear in print until after *Tay John* was published. His whole corpus is the product of the yarns he heard and the experiences he had as a young man; his writing life was a continual dipping back into a bran tub of stories gathered much earlier and only gradually moulded into written form. I intend, in the following pages, to trace the early stages of this process, and then to discuss its flowering in *Tay John*.


I


Jack Denham seems to have been a historical figure. In "The Writer That CanLit Forgot," which was based on an interview with O'Hagan towards the end of his life, Gary Geddes preserves a valuable account of the evolution of the novel:

He remembers walking on the hills back of Berkeley, aware that he could go no farther with the omniscient point of view in *Tay John*. Suddenly, he heard the voice of a local marine editor named

74

Jack Denham talking to him, telling him about Tay John and his dealings with the white man and his Iron Horse. (87)

By transporting Denham to the Canadian Rockies, O'Hagan makes him one with characters such as "Old" MacNamara and Montana Pete to whom he had listened a decade or more earlier. At this point, we can watch oral tale at the very instant of metamorphosis into written literature.

Earlier examples of the same process may be found in the two chapters of the 1958 edition of *Wilderness Men* that clearly reveal their oral origins: "The Black Ghost" and "Montana Pete Goes Courting." Both are set in a narrative frame in which the typical storytelling situation is reproduced: a wilderness man tells a tale to a listener who is a version of the young O'Hagan. In "The Black Ghost," set in 1920, "Old" MacNamara, ever in retreat before an encroaching civilization, is presented as spending his summers working on odd jobs at Lucerne on the shores of Yellowhead Lake (one of the main settings of *Tay John*), and his winters with his trap lines at a remote cabin "on the head of the Grantbrook" (13). A doctor's son, "a seventeen-year-old youth locally called 'Slim' who was home from his studies at McGill University" (15), succeeds in striking up a friendship with the old man, and is invited to accompany him on an expedition into the bush. As they hike over the mountains or sit around their camp fire by the cabin, the old man tells two stories: one of "The Thing That Walked like a Man" (19), a shadowy and unexplained presence that provides the subject for a disturbing ghost story; and one of a frightening encounter with a wolverine that belongs, for the literary categorizer, to the animal-story tradition.

"Montana Pete Goes Courting" contains three yarns: one is a traditional Indian tale (it recalls the opening section of *Tay John*), one explains the story's title, and one is about a lost horse. The last-mentioned narrative is a brief and rather inconsequential sketch of some four pages, but it is subsequently set within a framework by the following statement: "In January 1934, Montana Pete received a visit from a friend of construction days. It was then that he told the story of the white horse" (227). The friend in question was "Major Fred Brewster of Jasper, first world war veteran and the well-known guide and outfitter" (228) — a historical figure whom O'Hagan knew well, and who is mentioned by name in several of his writings, including *Tay*

*John* (206). Brewster, we are told, was accompanied by an Argentinian newspaperman, and the visit provided the occasion for Montana Pete's stories.

These two chapters, each consisting of unrelated yarns, are doubtless intended to reflect the casualness of their autobiographical source. O'Hagan, in his foreword, admits to a more personal role in the original situations that gave rise to the stories:

> I was the "doctor's son" who went with "Old" Macnamara up the ghostly Grantbrook in Chapter 1 and with Major Fred Brewster and the Argentine newspaperman visiting Montana Pete in Chapter 9. . . . The device of the third person was used to preserve the same point of view throughout the book. (6)

In the case of "Montana Pete Goes Courting," O'Hagan was clearly dissatisfied with the original version. Much of the material was reworked in later short stories — which explains why, when Talonbooks reprinted *Wilderness Men* in 1978, they omitted this chapter, since the material had already appeared in their enlarged edition of *The Woman Who Got On at Jasper Station* the previous year. The story of Montana Pete's courting is simply separated from its frame to become an incident told by an unidentified first-person narrator in the short story "The Tepee." But the tale of the missing horse is totally transformed.

In "The White Horse" (which appeared for the first time in the 1963 edition of *The Woman Who Got On at Jasper Station*), the storytelling frame has again been abandoned, and the protagonist is renamed Nick Durban. More interesting is the change of focus within the narrative, a change that has profound connections with some of the dominant concerns in *Tay John*. The original sketch is a simple tale of an old man who goes out seeking his equally aged horse, which has strayed. He eventually finds the horse frozen to death, and sadly leaves its body to the wolves. For no compelling reason, Montana Pete had named the horse Bedford after an English surveyor for whom he had once worked. This is no more than an undeveloped detail in the original sketch; but in "The White Horse," naming has become the principal subject.

Despite the new title, the horse's death is no longer the central concern. What was once a straightforward yarn has developed into a complex short story. Nick Durban, like Montana Pete, sets out to look for Bedford in "the High Valley," but, unlike Pete, he begins brooding on the name — and upon names in general:

It was called the High Valley for some reason that Nick could never understand for it was no more than a sloping tangle of jack-pine and down-timber. Yet, on the whole, poor though the name might be, he was glad that it had one. It was more home-like and warmer to have names about. In the valley only the creek was named and one mountain, called Black Mountain. All the hills were nameless. Even the pass which Nick crossed several times a year, leading into town and the railroad, was without a proper name. (56)

Nick discusses the matter with his friend Olaf the Swede (who, incidentally, had already made a brief appearance in *Tay John* [182]). Olaf "had said that in the old country all such places had names, but he did not see how, in these foothills a pass, especially a low, gentle pass, that had no name, would acquire one" (56). Within this context, the story of the naming of the horse after the surveyor takes on a little more meaning.

This meaning is developed considerably as the story continues. The discovery of the dead horse reminds Nick of his age and mortality. On going back to his cabin and rereading the "In Memoriam" and "Lost and Found" notices in the newspapers he uses to keep out the drafts, he is moved by "the idea of posting a reward to indicate you had lost what was important" (61). With great difficulty, he paints a sign announcing the loss of the horse and nails it to a tree, where trapper friends, including Olaf, would be sure to see it. Some weeks later, on passing the notice, Nick reads the tracks of previous travellers and follows one set towards "the pass without a name" (61). There he finds that Olaf, in response to his own notice, has erected a sign christening the place "Bedford Pass."

The narrative has evolved, then, into a probing story about the ways in which individuals and animals — and even stories — are remembered. Nick has performed a creator's part in giving Bedford his name (naming, we begin to realize, is a creative act, like storytelling); now Olaf has commemorated the incident by extending the name to the pass itself. Nick does not sentimentalize. He knows that the origins of names are soon forgotten, but also that they nurture and perpetuate developing myths.

Afterwards, the time would come when no one would remember. It would be a name, as the High Valley was a name. . . . Then the name would sink into the earth and become part of it. Nick, the first man to cross Bedford Pass, pointed his snowshoes down hill to town and the railroad where Olaf had gone before him. Bedford was now a name. The wolves would not have him. He would outlast flesh and bone and hide and hair. He would endure so long as men climbed rivers to their source and spoke into the wind the pass's name they travelled. (64–65)

It seems clear that O'Hagan finds value in the narratives of wilderness men who preserve memories of significant events and adventures that would otherwise be lost. At the same time, he realizes that literature demands more than a mere record of actions. When O'Hagan's yarns grow into stories, they take on a philosophical cast, and this is generally achieved through the development of a storyteller who meditates upon the implications of the tale he tells, and so teases the reader into an interpretation that extends beyond the literal. Within O'Hagan's work, the process finds its most complete embodiment in *Tay John*.

## I I

Every story — the rough-edged chronicle of a personal destiny — having its source in a past we cannot see, and its reverberations in a future still unlived — man, the child of darkness, walking for a few short moments in unaccustomed light — every story only waits, like a mountain in an untravelled land, for someone to come close, to gaze upon its contours, lay a name upon it, and relate it to the known world. (166–67)

This is one of the most frequently quoted sentences from *Tay John*, but it is worth considering again if only because it begins with story and ends with naming. No such passage appears in the earlier yarns, and only the faintest hint of such an approach occurs in the opening part of *Tay John* itself. A whole theory of comparative religion might be said to lie behind the presentation of Indian legend, replete with allusions outward to Judeo-Christian and Greek mythology, but this is assumed and available, never argued or asserted. Similarly, an aesthetic of narrative exists in "Hearsay," and Jack Denham is its spokesman. Tay John's story exists, as Denham says, "independently of me" (166), but to be a story rather than just a yarn it requires a thoughtful interpreter to tell it in an appropriate way, to trace it through its Indian and white manifestations, to set it within an intellectual context, and, above all, to name it by placing it within a lexicon of names and so render it permanent — or, at least, as permanent as anything can be "in men's time" (11).[1]

*Tay John* is so eclectic a book that it would be unwise to assume any single origin for the inspiration that led to its growth, but one of its origins was surely the names "Yellowhead Lake" and "Tête Jaune Cache." Unlike "The White Horse" and several other stories in *The Woman Who Got On at Jasper Station* (notably "The Bride's Crossing"), *Tay John* offers an explanation for an existing name rather than an account of how the name came into existence. The standard story is given in Milton and Cheadle's *The North-West Passage by Land* (1865) — a book that O'Hagan knew well, since he quotes from it twice in *Wilderness Men* (21, 250) and claimed to Geddes that its authors' anecdote and illustration concerning the headless Indian "provided the stimulus for the novel" (87). Milton and Cheadle explain (on the same page they offer the description of Mount Robson that O'Hagan quotes) that "The Grand Fork of the Fraser is the original Tête Jaune Cache, so called from being the spot chosen by an Iroquois trapper, known by the *sobriquet* of the Tête Jaune or 'Yellow Head,' to hide the furs he obtained on the western side" (257).

This is the generally accepted version, and in *Wilderness Men* O'Hagan offers a similar account (12). In *Tay John* itself, however, he alters the story for his own purpose:

> the Shuswaps were sometimes called the *Tête Jaune*, or Yellow-head people, and the place where they lived was known as *Tête Jaune Cache*, from their belief that one day a leader would come among them — a tall man (for they were of short stature) with yellow hair, and lead them back over the mountains to their cousins, the Salish tribes along the coast. (21–22)

Though he knows that the legend of Tay John is set in the past (recent research, according to Alan Rayburn, indicates that he was a mixed-blood Iroquois named Pierre Bostonais who died in 1827), O'Hagan chooses to set it in the period of the building of the railways (1880–1914).

In addition to changing Tay John from an Iroquois to a Shuswap, O'Hagan gives him a miraculous birth borrowed from a Tsimshian legend. The story of the Indian child's appearance out of the grave of his mother is adapted — sometimes word for word — from a passage in Diamond Jenness's *The Indians of Canada* (197–99).[2] This fact is of particular interest in view of the account of the growth of story I have offered in the previous section. Here the immediate source is written rather than oral (though it obviously had an oral origin), but for O'Hagan it provides a suitable beginning for his mythic hero. Its interest for my purpose is threefold. First, Indian story coexists equally in the novel with white story, reminding us that O'Hagan was one of the first writers to introduce Indians and Métis into his fiction without either idealization or condescension. Second, O'Hagan introduces names into Jenness's story — Hanni, Swamas, Kwakala, Smutuksen, and so on — as if to make the point that, when yarn or folktale evolves into fiction, names become essential. Third, while Jenness's version exists as a separate and discrete tale, under O'Hagan's hands it grows into a larger whole.

Part 1 of *Tay John*, "Legend," is packed with Indian lore. O'Hagan was obviously a scrupulous man and, since Jenness's book is the only written source he specifically acknowledges, we may safely assume that he picked up the rest of his material in the same way that he learned the stories from "Old" MacNamara and Montana Pete, by listening to Indian companions on the trail and around camp fires. In the prefatory note, O'Hagan makes reference not only to Jenness's book, but also to Professor Charles Hill-Tout, who gave him advice on the habits of local Indian tribes; he also acknowledges debts to "my friends, Jonnie Moyé and Joe Sangré of Fish Lake, near Brulé, Alberta, for many tales of their life and their people." Here, we may be confident, is the source of the rest of the Indian lore. One detail, however, is worth noting as a further example of O'Hagan's eclecticism. The girl about whom Tay John fights with Memhaias in the scene that leads to his exile from the tribe is named Shwat, and this is the name of the woman whose resistance led to the death of Tzouhalem, the Cowichan outlaw whose story, derived once again from oral tradition, is told in *Wilderness Men*. And in that book O'Hagan comments: "Somehow it seems fitting that the woman-avenger . . . went by the simple and compelling name of 'Shwat'" (221).

In part 1, then, O'Hagan has enlarged upon Jenness by giving the Indians names, but, for the most part, no particular significance is attached to them. Tay John himself, of course, has a number of names: he is first called Kumkan-Kleseem, then Kumkleseem "for his yellow head" (40); it is the visiting white men who christen him Tête Jaune, which is later slurred into Tay John (55), and so, as Arnold E. Davidson has noted, becomes "a purely conventional appellation instead of a partly descriptive one" (30). But as soon as we move to part 2, "Hearsay," the power of names becomes an immediate preoccupation, and, as in "The White Horse," is associated with storytelling. The first sentence reads: "In the year 1904, and in the years that followed, a new name blew up against the mountains, and an idea stirred like a wind through the valleys" (73). The name in question is "The Grand Trunk Pacific," and the link between "name" and "idea" is important. A few pages later, the survey-crew members (Jack Denham is one) are described as "men carried on the wind of an idea. They found themselves blown up a canyon where man had never been and words never lived before. Nameless river water tugged their saddle stirrups" (75). And at this point, we are introduced to Denham and his tale in the passage quoted at the beginning of this essay. Denham, like Conrad's Marlow, is a homespun philosopher as well as a wilderness man, and it is he who provides, within the framework of the story, thoughts about names similar to those that lie behind O'Hagan's expansion of Montana Pete's yarn into "The White Horse":

> It is physically exhausting to look on unnamed country. A name is the magic to keep it within the horizons. Put a name to it, put it on a map, and you've got it. The unnamed — it is the darkness unveiled. (80)

O'Hagan has subtly prepared us for our arrival at the setting of this comment. Denham is making his way up a "valley, with no name" (80), in an area where there are "any number of unnamed streams" (79). Unwittingly, he is travelling up the valley towards vision, and his journey is the white man's equivalent to that traditional Indian journey Tay John undertook in part 1. The vision that Denham has is of Tay John fighting the bear (his totem), and the thoughtful reader will realize at this point that the country is unnamed only from the white viewpoint, that Tay John and his fellow Indians may well have "[p]ut a name to it" and "got it" in their own speech. The fact that Tay John's very name was assigned to him by white men is significant, but it comes full circle when we realize that, according to O'Hagan's proleptic tradition, "Yellowhead" and "Tête Jaune Cache," though words in the white man's language, commemorate an Indian (or, at least, a part-Indian).

The novel that carries Tay John's name can therefore be seen as a medium for his power and the power of the myth that he represents (and that Michael Ondaatje celebrates in a pioneering article, "O'Hagan's Rough-Edged Chronicle").

The preoccupation with names is maintained throughout the novel. Solomon's Flats, where Tay John cuts off his hand, is named after "an old Indian chief who hunted there many years ago" (93). Dobble, the modern entrepreneur, thinks that names can be changed arbitrarily for commercial advantage. He forecasts that the name Yellowhead "will be forgotten in a year, two years," and that "the whole region will be known as the Switzerland of America" (171). He imports the name Lucerne, and it catches on, at least temporarily, but the whole novel is dedicated to the insistence that names are created in response to the people and events that become associated with them. The peak upon which Father Rorty dies almost immediately becomes "The Priest's Mountain" (223). Tay John plays out his destiny against the landscape and the names that anticipate his memorial.

We are witness, then, to the humanization, through names, of the landscape, and to the growth of legend and story. McLeod mentions "some sort of a story" or "legend" surrounding Tay John (99), and we are soon exposed to the process of distortion that is part of such storytelling. The tourist Arthur Alderson reports: "We had heard of Tay John down the line — of that yellow head, and of his losing his hand in a fight with a grizzly bear" (128). The official version within the novel (Denham's version) reads differently, but it is an essential part of the fictional effect (O'Hagan's effect) that the story should *not* be fixed permanently, that it should grow and develop like an organism. McLeod, therefore, does not demur at this new legend, and Denham gives us the alternative version without comment in the context of his own. And, finally, Denham rounds off the story with a report from Blackie the trapper, the last person to see Tay John alive. Thus Blackie's tale appropriately completes "Jackie's Tale" (notice how even tales are named). Blackie is himself a wilderness man like "Old" Macnamara and Montana Pete. He, too, has only one name, and among the tales he "garnered with his furs" is one of "wolverines that could outwit a man" (259), which recalls Macnamara's yarn in "The Black Ghost." And his account of Tay John walking down "under the snow and into the ground" (264) connects with a number of other passages in O'Hagan's fiction (including a closing passage in "The White Horse" that was previously quoted), notably Montana Pete's last sight of Felix Lapierre, in what was later to become "The Tepee": it was "as though he had walked down among the roots, under the faded grasses, into the earth, to which he was closer neighbor than I" (*Wilderness Men* 242; cf. *The Woman Who Got On at Jasper Station* 18).[3]

♦ ♦ ♦

*Tay John* was published in 1939. Two years later, Hugh MacLennan's *Barometer Rising* appeared, a novel often credited with the distinction of being the first Canadian novel set in an authentic (and named) Canadian city. O'Hagan deserves a place, with MacLennan and Sinclair Ross (to name two), among those writers considered to be pioneers of Canadian fiction, because he showed the way towards including native legend, the fact of western settlement, and the connection between naming and storytelling within the Canadian literary tradition. Above all, he demonstrated how stories can grow and evolve as they pass from one teller to another. I have documented this within O'Hagan's own fiction, but it happens, of course, from writer to writer as well. To take but two instances, the factual accounts of Almighty Voice and Albert Johnson in *Wilderness Men* provide part of the documentary basis for imaginative transformations of the incidents by Rudy Wiebe in his stories "Where is the Voice Coming From?" and "The Naming of Albert Johnson" (the latter growing later, in typical O'Hagan fashion, into Wiebe's novel *The Mad Trapper*). And Robert Harlow, in a section of his novel *Scann*, enlarges upon "Old" Macnamara's story of the wolverine in much the same way that O'Hagan turns the opening of "Montana Pete Goes Courting" into "The White Horse." It is not too much to say that Howard O'Hagan found a form in which the history of the elusive, because growing, Canadian West could be appropriately chronicled.

NOTES

[1] Both Davidson and Margery Fee stress the temporary or transitory nature of both naming and mythmaking in O'Hagan's fictional world.

[2] Jenness's account enables us to correct an absurd misprint in the text of *Tay John* (both the 1939 and 1960 editions). In the account of Swamas's visit to his wife's grave, one sentence reads: "On the grave he saw a small boy gathering

firewood" (36; pagination is the same in all published versions of the novel). This makes no sense, but the equivalent passage in Jenness resolves the difficulty: "As he drew near it he saw a little boy gathering fireweed . . ." (197).

3 Although the relation between short story and novel is not altogether clear, *The School-Marm Tree* seems to have developed in a similar manner. The image of its title first appears in *Tay John*, where Father Rorty crucifies himself on "a school-marm tree" (217); the short story "The School-Marm Tree" (which appears only in the 1963 edition of *The Woman Who Got On at Jasper Station*) consists of an incident in which such a tree is central, and the novel of the same name expands the account of the chief character, Selva Williams, still further. The settings include, once again, Yellowhead and the High Valley.

### WORKS CITED

Davidson, Arnold E. "Silencing the Word in Howard O'Hagan's *Tay John*." *Canadian Literature* 110 (1986): 31–44.

Fee, Margery. "Howard O'Hagan's *Tay John*: Making New World Myth." *Canadian Literature* 110 (1986): 8–27.

Geddes, Gary. "The Writer That CanLit Forgot." *Saturday Night* Nov. 1977: 84–92.

Jenness, Diamond. *The Indians of Canada*. 7th ed. Toronto: U of Toronto P, 1977.

Milton, William Fitzwilliam (Viscount), and Walter Butler Cheadle. *The North-West Passage by Land; Being the Narrative of an Expedition from the Atlantic to the Pacific*. Toronto: Coles, 1970.

O'Hagan, Howard. *Tay John*. 1960. New Canadian Library 105. Toronto: McClelland, 1989.

——. *The School-Marm Tree*. Vancouver: Talonbooks, 1977.

——. *Wilderness Men*. Garden City, NY: Doubleday, 1958.

——. *The Woman Who Got On at Jasper Station and Other Stories*. 1963. Rev. and enl. ed. Vancouver: Talonbooks, 1977.

Ondaatje, Michael. "O'Hagan's Rough-Edged Chronicle." *Canadian Literature* 61 (1974): 24–31.

Rayburn, Alan. "Great Divide Passes in the Rockies." *Canadian Geographic* Apr.–May 1986: 88–89.

# A Note on the Publishing History of Howard O'Hagan's *Tay John*

MARGERY FEE

Laidlaw and Laidlaw (until 1938 Laidlaw and Butchart), once of 32 Alfred Place, London, WC 1, disappeared shortly after publishing Howard O'Hagan's *Tay John*. It is not clear whether they marched off to war, were bombed, or simply folded. The following Laidlaw and Laidlaw publications are listed in their edition of *Tay John*: Donald Armour's *Swept and Garnished* (1938), Robert MacLaughlin's *The Axe Fell: The Story of the Cenci* (1938), Charles Bromfield's *To Walk Alone* (1939), Kenneth Gee's *The Dead Can't Hurt You* (1938), Edna O'Brien's *So I Went to Prison* (1938), Margaret Thomsen Raymond's *Sylvia, Inc.* (1938), Boyne Grainger's *The Jester's Reign* (1938), and Ezra Pound's *Gaudier-Brzeska* [1939].

Whatever the fate of Laidlaw and Laidlaw, their 1939 edition of *Tay John* provided the plates for Clarkson N. Potter's 1960 edition, and the Potter edition provided the plates for McClelland and Stewart's 1974 and 1989 reprints. A careful look at the Potter edition reveals darker type where revisions were made within the lines, either by an editor or, as seems most likely, by O'Hagan himself.[1] To Laidlaw and Laidlaw's credit, none of the revisions are obviously of misprints. Since publishers prefer to avoid the expense of such painstaking typesetting work for the sake of almost imperceptible changes in effect, it seems almost certain that O'Hagan was the source of the revisions. The fact that Clarkson N. Potter was O'Hagan's agent and friend (at least until problems with the Potter contract became clear) may explain why O'Hagan was allowed to do so much tinkering.

All of these changes are listed at the end of this article. Some seem to have been made simply to Americanize the text; for example, a reference to Charles's Wain has been changed to The Big Dipper (220; page references are the same in all published versions of the text), and "back-cloth" has become "back-drop" (85). Other alterations seem to have been made in order to render details more concrete; so for example, the Laidlaw edition's "some horses," has been changed to "four horses" in the Potter edition (15; and see 14, 22). Twice in the 1939 version, horses wander off in search of "feeding"; this has been changed to "feed" in the 1960 edition (13, 119). One change seems to have required some knowledge, although not necessarily on O'Hagan's part: the "carrots" the Shuswap bake in the 1939 edition are "parsnips" in that of 1960 (22). A change that might have been made by an editor interested in simplifying the text, or perhaps by the author, occur in a description of Tay John's face: "It was in his face, too, long and keen as though shaped by the wind, and beardless as a boy's — those fellows (*'huch'* they are called) — seldom if ever have a beard" (83). The 1960 edition removes the parenthetical comment and what follows and replaces it with: "those fellows — I could see he was of mixed blood — are often lightly bearded" (83).

Several changes, however, seem to be of the sort that only an author would care or dare to make. For example, the first line of the novel changes from "The time of this *at* its beginning, in men's time" (1939) to "The time of this *in* its beginning, in men's time" (1960). The change moves the reader from the linear narrative of realism to the multilevel narrative of myth, where time is no longer a line, but an abyss. Echoed is the beginning of another work: "In the beginning was the Word and the Word was with God, and the Word was God" (John 1.1). In John is also an allusion to what will become one of the controlling symbolic oppositions of the novel: "And the light shineth in darkness; and the darkness comprehended it not" (John 1.5). In the first chapter of his gospel, John talks of a man who comes ahead, who is not the Messiah, who describes himself as "the voice of one crying in the wilderness" (1.23). *Tay John* contains the stories of the coming of several men to the Shuswap people and their land, such as Red Rorty, Father Rorty, Alf Dobble, and Tay John himself. All the stories of these men echo or parody the story of a leader sent by God, although none finally fulfills the promise. Jackie Denham, like John, has a gospel, a tall tale that he tells in the wilderness.

Another change that seems likely to have been authorial has been made to Tay John's account of his "spirit quest," during which, he reports, an old bear had slept near him, "for in the morning he left his shape *and shreds of fur* behind him" (49; emphasis added to show alterations to manuscript). The added image ties in with O'Hagan's frequent allusions to hair: Tay John's remarkable head of gold, the hair of mountain goats or horses, or the fleece of sheep caught on trees — a trace of passage. Yet another example may be found where words have been added to the end of a sentence: ". . . it was a strong belief and gave its name to their district *and, in English, to the pass to the east*" (22; emphasis added to indicate added words). This change fits with the actual toponymy of the Yellowhead region. O'Hagan's detailed knowledge of the mountain terrain, and the importance he placed on getting it right, is again reflected in a revision of the location of Grande Cache (95). There are other minor revisions that seem likely to be authorial: Red Rorty does not kneel before "the" mountain in the 1960 edition, but before "a" mountain (23), and the rhythm has been improved in the sentence "Without a name no man is an individual, no individual a man" by the addition of the word "wholly": the 1960 edition reads, "no individual *wholly* a man" (87). The deletion of one letter from another passage completely alters its meaning. In the 1939 edition, "Kwakala, a man great in his magic, who cursed with his songs and his beaver-tooth rattle," "cures" with these things in the 1960 edition (25). This change creates an image that better fits the man's character.

Further, the second edition omits an introductory quotation, which apparently came from a San Francisco newspaper, and adds Harvey Fergusson's introduction (included in the 1974 McClelland and Stewart reprint, but dropped in the 1989 one). Although O'Hagan has maintained in profiles and interviews that he had never heard of a man cutting off his own hand (Roberts 45–46; see also Keith Maillard's interview with O'Hagan in this volume), the first edition contains, on the page facing the opening lines of chapter 7, the following extract, which may have inspired a central incident in the novel:

PRISONER USES AXE
TO CHOP OFF
HIS HAND
San Francisco, July 30
   From Alcatraz Island came a story that one of the convicts in the prison had deliberately chopped off his own hand with an axe. The prisoner was named only as "Percival."
   Secretly obtaining an axe, he filed the edge to razor-sharpness.

Then, a report says, he held the axe in his right hand and with a single stroke chopped off the left.

He is said to have handed the axe to another prisoner with the plea: "Cut off my right hand."

The second convict called guards.

James Johnston, warden of the federal institution, would neither deny nor confirm the story.

Fergusson's introduction is one of the main sources of the myth of Howard O'Hagan as uncomplicated mountain man, a myth that persists into contemporary criticism. Fergusson's name, either from his novels or from his Hollywood screenplays, was familiar to American readers,[2] but would have done nothing to promote *Tay John* in Great Britain.

O'Hagan spent the last years of his life trying to regain the copyright to his most famous novel.[3] The contract he had with Clarkson Potter lacked the customary reversion clause, that is, the clause that stipulates that if a work is out of print for a designated length of time, normally a year or less, the copyright reverts to the author. Clarkson Potter published 4,000 copies in 1960, at $4.50 a copy. By 1965, the book was out of print, whether through sales or through remaindering is not clear. In 1974, McClelland and Stewart acquired Canadian paperback rights. For these they paid Clarkson Potter. O'Hagan said he received no royalties in his lifetime from these Canadian sales, although his contract with Clarkson Potter did oblige the publisher to pay them. Possibly, during the time to which O'Hagan refers, the owed royalties had still failed to offset an advance Potter paid to O'Hagan for the 1960 edition. Like other Canadian writers, such as Hugh MacLennan, O'Hagan found that his sales in Canada increased his fame far more than his bank balance.

♦ ♦ ♦

What follows is a list of changes to the 1939 edition. When a change was made, the whole line was generally replaced. In the list, I reproduce the entire line from the 1939 edition only. Where it seems helpful, the changed word or words have been italicized in the line quoted from the 1939 edition. Although the difference in the darkness of type cannot be seen very clearly in the McClelland and Stewart reprints, the lines in

them are identical to those in the 1960 edition, and those who do not
have access to the first and second editions, which are fairly scarce, can
use the reprints to set the text below in context.

PAGE/LINE

11/1   1939  The time of this *at* its beginning, in men's time
       1960              in

13/7   1939  there was game and fish, *feeding* for their horses, and
       1960                            feed

14/17  1939  edge of the clearing, *half a mile* from his door, was
       1960                         ninety yards

15/6   1939  Athabaska Valley with *some horses* and the money he
       1960                         four horses

16/1   1939  Christian soldiers," and *"Brighten the corner where*
 /2          *you are."*
       1960                            "Bright With All His Crowns"

22/6   1939  district.
       1960  district and, in English, to the pass to the east.

22/19  1939  and *carrots*, which they baked in an oven under the
       1960      parsnips

22/25  1939  Red Rorty walked for *many* days to come to them,
       1960                        three

22/27  1939  longer steady and he found game hard to *seek* with his
       1960                                           hit

23/1   1939  grew along the trail. Sometimes he knelt before *the*
       1960                                                   a

25/15  1939  Kwakala, a man great in his magic, who *cursed* with
       1960                                         cured

47/22  1939  face grown lean and hard with his journey gleamed
       1960  [comma added after "journey"]  ,

89

| | | |
|---|---|---|
| 49/23 /24 | 1939 | watch me, for in the morning he left his shape behind him." |
| | 1960 | he left his shape and shreds of fur behind him." |
| 80/17 | 1939 | he would have surprised *a creator* at his work — for a |
| | 1960 | the Creator |
| 83/17 | 1939 | ties that *all* men search for. It was in his face, too, long |
| | 1960 | ["all" has been deleted] |
| 83/19 /20 | 1939 | as a boy's — those fellows (*'huch'* they are called) — seldom if ever have a beard. I felt I was an intruder, |
| | 1960 | — those fellows — I could see he was of mixed blood — are often lightly bearded. |
| 85/3 /4 | 1939 | my benefit, with the forest and mountains for back-cloth |
| | 1960 | drop |
| 87/4 | 1939 | name no man is an individual, no individual a man. |
| | 1960 | no individual wholly a man. |
| 92/15 /16 | 1939 | light, making the silence about me something that I could see — and hear. |
| | 1960 | making the silence about me visible. ["something I could see — and hear" has been deleted] |
| 95/8 | 1939 | of dark-skinned hill people, descendents of Crees of |
| | 1960 | and of |
| 95/11 | 1939 | at Grande Cache, more than a hundred miles *north* of |
| | 1960 | west on |
| 96/8 | 1939 | sides the grass was *for ever* green, the trees eternally in |
| | 1960 | forever |
| 119/2 | 1939 | legs, will wander far off the trail in search of *feeding* — |
| | 1960 | feed |
| 119/9 | 1939 | but Tay John did not return until summer *passed* and |
| | 1960 | had passed |
| 213/17 | 1939 | behind *us*? I was on my knees so I could not see |
| | 1960 | you? |

214/27 1939 candle, moving great upon the wall above me, the
       1960 candle, moving great upon the wall. Above me, the

220/11 1939 Stars shone for a time. *Charles' Wain* wheeled
       1960                         The Big Dipper

236/26 1939 on a hillside, tail sucked between his legs — darkness
    /27      made visible.
       1960 ["darkness made visible" has been deleted, and a full
            stop added after "legs"]

245/9 1939 saddles, had gone *on in* the freight the day before.
      1960                in on

NOTES

¹ I thank Chris Petter for pointing out the darker type to me, and for explaining what it meant.

² Robert Gish's biography of Harvey Fergusson, although it contains only a few passing references to O'Hagan, does cast some light on the California writing milieu they shared.

³ I thank Karl Siegler of Talonbooks for telling me what he knew of O'Hagan's attempt to recover his copyright.


WORKS CITED

Gish, Robert. *Frontier's End: The Life and Literature of Harvey Fergusson*. Lincoln: U of Nebraska P, 1988.

O'Hagan, Howard. *Tay John*. London: Laidlaw, 1939.

——. *Tay John*. New York: Potter, 1960.

Roberts, Kevin. "Talking to Howard O'Hagan." *Event* 5 (1976): 41–48.

# Ethnographic Notes on Howard O'Hagan's *Tay John*

**RALPH MAUD**

In a preliminary statement to *Tay John*, Howard O'Hagan expressed his indebtedness to Diamond Jenness for his book *The Indians of Canada*, to Professor Charles Hill-Tout, and to two Métis of his acquaintance. His intention in citing these sources was to authenticate the passages in the novel purporting to render the life and customs of the Native people. It can readily be confirmed that his claim to ethnographic validity is, on the whole, sound.

The name Tay John is derived from the Native guide who, in 1820, took the first Hudson's Bay party through what is now called Yellowhead Pass. According to the Akriggs's *British Columbia Place Names*, this guide, Pierre Hatsinaton, had been given the nickname "Tête Jaune," presumably because of his light-coloured hair (301). He was probably an Iroquois, as a band of these eastern Natives had entered the region with fur trappers in the early years of the century, and, according to James Teit's authoritative study *The Shuswap*, had settled exactly at Tête Jaune Cache in the northeast corner of Shuswap country, at the headwaters of the Fraser River (468). O'Hagan gives his own "Tête Jaune" an alien status reminiscent of that of the historical outsider.

Perhaps it was from his Métis informants that O'Hagan got the notion that the Shuswap believed "that one day a leader would come among them . . . with yellow hair and lead them back over the mountains to their cousins, the Salish tribes along the coast" (21–22). Nothing in the written sources on the subject suggests that the Shuswap have, or had, a nostalgia for the coast. O'Hagan may have been tapping the universal archetype of the messiah, which may also be traced in the Aztec myth of the fair-skinned Quetzalcoatl.

In any case, it is clear that O'Hagan felt that his hero should have an extraordinary beginning, like other mythic heroes. He appropriated a

Tsimshian legend for this purpose. He found the story in Diamond Jenness's *The Indians of Canada* (197–99), and followed it quite closely in the novel (35–39). It tells of a child miraculously being born from a dead mother. In other versions, the child nurtures himself from the mother's corpse, and Franz Boas, in his *Tsimshian Mythology*, gives the title "Sucking Intestines" to the motif (214).[1] Though O'Hagan tells it matter-of-factly, it is a macabre tale, and serves to endow the personality of Tay John with a rather chilling quality.

Jenness could have been the source (if anything beyond the novelist's own observation were needed) for the description of the general culture of the Shuswap — camping, hunting, and the vision quest. O'Hagan's indebtedness to Jenness is strikingly revealed in a detail or two. Jenness writes, "when the tribe moved camp he [the elder in charge of the young men] sometimes held them back for two or three hours and forced them to race the whole distance to the new settlement" (153). In O'Hagan's novel, when the camp was moved, the young Tay John "waited till the others had gone far [so] that, running to overtake them, his legs would become hard" (44). The idea of the fight between Tay John and Memhaias may have been suggested by a sentence from Jenness: "The Athapaskans (and sometimes the Eskimo) even wrestled for each other's wives when these were good-looking, so that a strong man might arrogate to himself half a dozen young girls" (156).

Some details of the betrothal scene in *Tay John* appear in another source, James Teit's *The Thompson Indians of British Columbia*. In O'Hagan's novel, Memhaias touches Shwat's breasts and points an arrow at her belly, "for these were signs that the girl would understand" (64). Teit writes:

A man who touched the naked breasts or heel of a maiden transformed her at once into his wife, and there was no retraction for either party, so that henceforth they lived together as man and wife. If a young man intentionally touched a young woman with his arrow, it was the same as asking her to become his wife. (323–24)

So, according to this, Memhaias was doubly betrothed before Tay John "looked also upon Shwat," and in the middle of the village "lifted her skirt and ripped open her breech clout — for this, too, was a sign the girl would understand" (64). Teit indicates that to "cut her breech-cloth" was also a legitimate way of proposing to a maiden (*Thompson Indians* 324). Tay John's offense, therefore, is clearly not in his method, but in the fact that he contests the prior claim at all.

O'Hagan did not acknowledge his debt to Teit; this information may have come to him through Charles Hill-Tout, who knew Teit's work well. Hill-Tout paraphrases Teit's passages about the arrow and the "breech-cloth" in his book *British North America* (191). A further detail from this book is pertinent: "Another practice amongst the youths of the hunting-tribes was to lie all night on the bank or margin of a stream or lake, and keep the hands in the water" (246). This information is used in *Tay John* (44).

Alternatively, such details could have been gathered by O'Hagan in his personal conversation with Charles Hill-Tout (in the acknowledgment note, Hill-Tout is thanked for his "advice"), who was in Vancouver at the time O'Hagan was spending summers on Vancouver Island planning the novel. Indeed, Hill-Tout would have been the obvious choice for a consultant, being the local expert on, and popularizer of, Indian subjects, and the president of the Vancouver Art, Historical, and Scientific Society for the decade 1934–44.[2]

It seems likely that O'Hagan talked to Hill-Tout about an appropriate Indian name for Tay John in his youth. *K'womkEn*, the word for *head* in Hill-Tout's Lillooet word list,[3] could have given O'Hagan the first part of the name, "Kumkan" (40). The second part of the name, "Kleseem," turns up in Hill-Tout's "Report on the Ethnology of the Siciatl" as the Sechelt word for *yellow*: *k'lEsem* (91). Hill-Tout never published a Shuswap word list, and, in providing O'Hagan with "Head-Yellow," was improvising from the Indian languages he knew best.

One person who spent time among the Shuswap during the 1880s was George M. Dawson of the Geological Survey of Canada. O'Hagan might have seen his "Notes on the Shuswap People of British Columbia" in the *Proceedings and Transactions of the Royal Society of Canada* (1891). One paragraph is quite pertinent:

The Kamloops Indians affirm, that the very highest mountain they know is on the north side of the valley at Tête Jaune Cache, about ten miles from the valley. This is named *Yuh-hai-has'-kun*, from the appearance of a spiral road running up it. No one has ever been known to reach the top, though a former chief of Tsuk-tsukkwalk', on the North Thompson, was near the top once when hunting goats. When he realized how high he had climbed he became frightened and returned. (37)

This has a bearing on Tay John's journey up the "cruel" valley to obtain a guardian spirit (46–49). However, it is the kind of common lore about the Yellowhead Pass that O'Hagan might have heard from his friends Moyé and Sangré (the Métis whose help he acknowledges in his preliminary statement) of Brulé, on the Alberta side of the pass.

It would be invidious to go through every detail of the novel trying to discover whether O'Hagan was dependent on known sources. We have looked at the passages that deal most conspicuously with Indian culture and found them to be ethnographically reliable, at least sufficiently reliable to quell any unease that would make a reading of the novel less enjoyable.

## NOTES

[1] Jenness actually collected his version of the myth on a visit to the Carrier Indians in 1924 (see his "Myths of the Carrier Indians" 149–54). It is because of Boas's discussion in *Tsimshian Mythology* (781) that Jenness ascribes the myth to the Carriers' Tsimshian neighbours. Ironically, it was not known until later (see Krappe 313–14) that this "Tsimshian" story was originally a French fabliau brought into the Canadian West by early *coureurs de bois*.

[2] Hill-Tout's ethnographic reports have been collected, along with biographical information, in *The Salish People: The Local Contribution of Charles Hill-Tout* (1978).

[3] I am indebted to Randy Bouchard of the British Columbia Indian Language Project, Victoria, for confirming this linguistic point. The word in question is included in the list entitled "Parts of the Body" in Hill-Tout's "Report on the Ethnology of the Stlatlumh" (208).

## WORKS CITED

Akrigg, G.P.V., and Helen B. Akrigg. *British Columbia Place Names*. Victoria, BC: Sono Nis, 1986.

Boas, Franz. *Tsimshian Mythology*. 31st Annual Report of the Bureau of American Ethnology. Washington: Smithsonian Institute, 1916.

Dawson, George M. "Notes on the Shuswap People of British Columbia." *Proceedings and Transactions of the Royal Society of Canada* 9 (1891): 3–44.

Hill-Tout, Charles. *British North America I: The Far West; The Home of the Salish and Dene*. The Native Races of the British Empire. London: Constable, 1907.

———. "Report on the Ethnology of the Siciatl of British Columbia, a Coast Division of the Salish Stock." *Journal of the Royal Anthropological Institute* 34 (1904): 20–91.

———. "Report on the Ethnology of the Stlatlumh of British Columbia." *Journal of the Royal Anthropological Institute* 35 (1905): 126–218.

Jenness, Diamond. *The Indians of Canada*. National Museum of Canada Bulletin 65, Anthropological Series 15. Ottawa: Acland, 1932.

———. "Myths of the Carrier Indians of British Columbia." *Journal of American Folklore* 47 (1934): 97–257.

Krappe, Alexander H. "A Solomon Legend Among the Indians of the North Pacific." *Journal of American Folklore* 59 (1946): 309–14.

O'Hagan, Howard. *Tay John*. 1960. New Canadian Library 105. Toronto: McClelland, 1989.

Teit, James Alexander. *The Shuswap*. Ed. Franz Boas. 1909. New York: AMS Reprint, 1975. Vol. 2 [part 7] of *The Jesup North Pacific Expedition*.

———. *The Thompson Indians of British Columbia*. Ed. Franz Boas. New York: n.p., 1900. Vol. 1 [part 4] of *The Jesup North Pacific Expedition*.

# The Canonization of Two Underground Classics: Howard O'Hagan's *Tay John* and Malcolm Lowry's *Under the Volcano*

MARGERY FEE

Canonization is invariably an institutional project, and usually requires the support of most of the following: the writer; the writer's family and friends; those working in the same literary mode; agents; financial institutions that support writers; publishers; and the critical institution, including reviewers, teachers of literature, and scholars.[1] In 1939, when *Tay John* was published, the Canadian literary institution was not highly developed; although the 1920s had seen some rapid develop-ment, the Depression had taken its toll. Further, *Tay John* was published abroad, and was not promoted well. Still, when compared even to another underground classic, Malcolm Lowry's *Under the Volcano*, its canonization was exceptionally slow until 1974, and then, exception-ally fast. Although tracing the history of the reception and canonization of one work cannot answer all questions about the canonization process in a particular literary institution, an attempt to account for the 35-year neglect of *Tay John* in Canada, and its subsequent "discovery," does cast light on several of the many variables that play a part in the construction of the Canadian literary tradition. Perhaps the most interesting question to ask is why the novel was uniformly praised abroad and damned at home, at least for the first 35 years of its history.

Howard O'Hagan's novel *Tay John* was first published in London, in 1939, by a small firm called Laidlaw and Laidlaw. A slightly revised edition was published in 1960, in New York, by Clarkson N. Potter. Not until D.G. Jones mentioned the novel in *Butterfly on Rock* (1970), however, did it come to the attention of the Canadian literary institution in any positive sense. In 1974, Malcolm Ross published the first

McClelland and Stewart New Canadian Library Series reprint of *Tay John*. In the same year, George Woodcock reviewed the novel favourably in *Maclean's*, and Michael Ondaatje published an article on it in *Canadian Literature*. Margaret Atwood considered the novel at length in a lecture delivered at Harvard in 1976, a lecture published the following year in *The Canadian Imagination*, edited by David Staines.[2] All of this attention contributed to the appearance of *Tay John* as number 76 on the list of the most "important" works of fiction chosen by a group of Canadian teachers and critics in 1978 (Steele 153). In the eight years since Jones's discussion, *Tay John* had transcended a state of virtual oblivion, achieved a fairly secure place in the canon of Canadian fictional, and received the praise of some of the most important writers and critics in the country. O'Hagan had been made an honorary member of the Writers' Union of Canada, had been granted a Canada Council Senior Arts Bursary to write his memoirs, and had been given a honorary doctorate by McGill University. Several Canadian writers had supported the granting of these awards to O'Hagan, including Margaret Atwood, Gary Geddes, Robert Harlow, Margaret Laurence, Ken Mitchell, Michael Ondaatje, P.K. Page, and George Woodcock.

Although there is no evidence that the novel sold particularly well in England or the United States, *Tay John* had earlier been reviewed positively in all the right publications in both countries. In London in 1939, *Tay John* was reviewed in the *Times Literary Supplement*; the 200-word review concluded with the statement, "This is an odd, compelling story and one that is likely to live on in the mind." Frank Swinnerton of the London *Observer* praised the novel in his weekly column, "New Novels." Shortly afterwards (on 26 March), an advertisement appeared in the *Observer* quoting from the review and bearing the heading "A Novel of the Grey Owl Country." Grey Owl, whose name had been made with the publication of *Pilgrims of the Wild* (1935), had recently completed a reading tour of England, which culminated in an appearance before the royal family in April 1938. Both reviewers read *Tay John* in the context of Grey Owl's nature stories, Swinnerton remarking that the novel stirred "romantic longings," and the *TLS* reviewer accounting for the novel's disjunctions by reading it as a backwoods tale, "a mixture of the credible and the incredible."

In 1960 in the United States, the novel was reviewed in *Booklist*, the *Library Journal*, and in the Sunday *New York Times Book Review*. Richard Ohmann notes, in "The Shaping of a Canon: U.S. Fiction,

1960–75," that "[t]he single most important boost a novel could get was a prominent review in the Sunday *New York Times* — better a favorable one than an unfavorable one, but better an unfavorable one than none at all" (380). O'Hagan received a favourable review of 450 words.

In Canada, the novel was also reviewed in the journals whose readers were most likely to be interested in it. In 1939, the *Canadian Forum* devoted 69 words to Tay John, remarking that "One seems to have read it all many times before." Given this magazine's modernist leanings, its reviewers were unlikely to be entranced by anything that resembled a latter-day *Wacousta*, filled with the kind of melodrama and romance that critics were still trying to purge from the fictional canon. Nor would the Grey Owl angle appeal, since the animal story was, in Canada at least, old hat. For the *University of Toronto Quarterly*'s reviewer, J.R. MacGillivray, the two important Canadian novels of 1939 were both realist: Frederick Niven's *The Story of Their Days* and Frederick Philip Grove's *Two Generations*. MacGillivray took 40 words to conclude that *Tay John*, which he classed as a romance, was "confused and confusing in development and undistinguished in characterization."

In 1961, F.W. Watt devoted slightly less than twice as many words to saying much the same thing in the same place, the *University of Toronto Quarterly*. George Robertson, in *Canadian Literature*, did rather better, devoting 750 words to the novel. Robertson criticized O'Hagan for his "artifice," for "the strain, the consciousness of verbal elaboration [which] is an irritating presence between ourselves and the story . . . in the end we are always brought around to the author saying 'Here is myth in the making' " (65). The narrator, Jackie Denham, is seen as an "unsatisfactory pivot for the story," who seems to exist "to throw Tay John out of focus" (66). Robertson succinctly outlines all the features the contemporary poststructuralist critic likes, but damns them. He is unprepared to see Denham as a parodic version of Conrad's Marlow, whose role is to demonstrate that no one sees Tay John clearly. "Legend," Robertson declares, "whatever the mystery it enshrines, is never dim" (66). Contrast this with Stuart Keate's conclusion in the *New York Times*: "If Tay John emerges as a shadowy figure, it is all of a piece with the author's philosophy."

Another reason that only scant support was offered to O'Hagan is that the literary institution is generally national, rather than international. When O'Hagan published in England in 1939, he was unknown there; he wrote the novel in Berkeley, California and, in the summers, on the West Coast of Canada. His literary connections were mainly formed while he was at McGill University and in Berkeley. In 1960, when the novel was published in New York, the O'Hagans were on Vancouver Island. When the novel was reprinted in Toronto in 1974, O'Hagan had been in Italy for 10 years, and he only heard that it had been reprinted after his return. Canadian writers have succeeded in the United States and Great Britain. However, such success is not likely if a writer's literary connections with the place where his or her work is published are nonexistent, and if the subject matter of that work is emphatically Canadian. Any success *Tay John* did have seems to have come despite its author's inability to foster it.

In accounting for the uneasy and lukewarm reception of O'Hagan's *Tay John* in Canada between 1939 and 1970, a comparison with Malcolm Lowry's *Under the Volcano* (1947), also an underground classic, seems helpful, even inevitable. Lowry and O'Hagan were strikingly similar. Both wrote avant-garde works that rejected the bourgeois status quo. Indeed, both writers were extremely well educated, led Bohemian lives, and thus may also have been rejecting the expectations of their professional fathers. Both married beautiful artists they met in California; both lived and wrote on the West Coast of Canada. Indeed, in the late 1930s, both may well have been thrown out of the same bars in Mexico. Both lived in British Columbia, on the fringes of the universe in relation to the literary centres of New York, London, and even Toronto. At their one meeting, they did not get along. O'Hagan described the meeting to Kevin Roberts:

> He and I and A.J.M. Smith had a drink together. He wanted to talk about how wonderful it was to be a seaman. Very boring. I'd been a seaman and it's dull. Just chipping rust and painting and looking at the damn sea all the time. . . . [Lowry was] very patronizing. He said I had some nice descriptive pieces in *Tay John* and I said he had some pleasant descriptive pieces in *The Volcano*. (Roberts 47)

O'Hagan then ended the competition by quoting a descriptive passage from *War and Peace, the* canonical novel.

Despite all the similarities between the two authors, Lowry's novel was discovered much sooner and has done much better than O'Hagan's.

William H. New, in his introduction to *Malcolm Lowry: A Reference Guide* (1978), notes that "*Under the Volcano* won immediate response — enthusiastic in the United States, disparaging in England, and somewhat puzzled in Canada . . . (xiv)." He goes on to point out that, despite its underground status, it was a Book of the Month Club Choice, and was on the American best-seller lists for some time. In fact, one suspects that the label "underground" appealed to those readers who flaunted their tastes as antibourgeois; they were likely to uphold the label long after it was really outdated, if only to confirm the exclusivity of their taste. Indeed, by 1966, a reception study had been written tracing the novel's shift from underground to classic (Black), a shift confirmed by the increasing numbers of theses, dissertations, and books devoted to Lowry and his most famous novel. A simple explanation for the different receptions of O'Hagan and Lowry might be that Lowry wrote a better novel. But what is "better"? Nowadays, we cannot be quite so naïve about the constitution of the canon: as Pierre Bourdieu remarks, "a cultural product . . . is a constituted taste . . ." (231).

A close comparison of these novels' relation to the literary institutions of Great Britain, Canada, and the United States reveals some more specific reasons for the differences in the ways they were received. Lowry was fortunate to be taken on by the publishers Reynal and Hitchcock and Jonathan Cape, who published his novel in 1947, and O'Hagan emphatically was not lucky in this regard. *Tay John* was first published in 1939 in London, with a firm that published at least seven interesting works, including Ezra Pound's memoir of Gaudier-Brzeska and Edna O'Brien's *So I Went to Prison*, before disappearing. Clarkson N. Potter of New York printed 4,000 copies of the novel in 1960. This edition was reviewed at least six times, in three Canadian and three American publications. The firm apparently remaindered it without notifying O'Hagan, although they may have tried to reach him. In 1964, O'Hagan followed his wife, Margaret Peterson, to Italy. Supported by a Canada Council grant, she had gone to Italy to continue her work in mosaic.

Generally, authors have to promote their own careers, although a trustworthy agent can help. It also helps to have a spouse whose sole interest is one's career. Without Margerie Bonner Lowry, or someone like her, Lowry would have published little or nothing. Margaret Peterson O'Hagan was a well-established artist and a professor at Berkeley when she met O'Hagan, and quite justifiably saw her own artistic career as at least as important as his. Each thought highly of the other's abilities; she certainly supported him financially to some degree, and her paintings appear on the covers of those of O'Hagan's works that were published by Talonbooks. Neither, however, made much money from their art. Certainly Peterson was too busy to be the full-time literary support that Margerie Lowry was to her husband. Living in Italy from 1964 to 1974, O'Hagan was in no position to keep track of what was happening to his novel's royalties, let alone orchestrate its canonization.

Lowry obviously tied his novel to a world tradition, rather than to a Canadian one. (Although *Under the Volcano* is set in Mexico, its main characters are English or European.) Thus, once he was discovered, a wide audience was opened up for him. *Tay John* was obviously, even aggressively, Canadian. Unfortunately, Canadian critics who saw it as a wilderness novel would be likely to dismiss it as old-fashioned; those who tried to read it in the contemporary realist tradition dominated by Frederick Philip Grove and Morley Callaghan would be frustrated by its romantic and satiric elements. (Significantly, O'Hagan comments of Callaghan in a 1975 letter to George Woodcock: "That fellow, when I have tried to read him, leaves me with a sullen ache in the *posterior fundum*" [O'Hagan, Letter].)

Further, Lowry embraced the persona of the avant-garde writer and intellectual, while O'Hagan explicitly rejected it. When he received a Canada Council Senior Arts Bursary in 1976, his recorded comment was "not bad for an old horse handler." Margaret O'Hagan interjected, "Come on, Howard, You were a lawyer" (Roberts 45). Neither, typically, is quite telling the truth. One is reminded of Alice Munro's story "Material," in which the divorced wife of a writer mocks a blurb that appears on his short story collection:

> But listen to the lies, the half-lies, the absurdities. *He lives on the side of a mountain above Vancouver.* It sounds as if he lives in a wilderness cabin, and all it means, I'm willing to bet, is that he lives in an ordinary comfortable house in North or West Vancouver, which now stretch far up the mountain. . . . You would think he came out of the bush now and then to fling them scraps of wisdom. . . . (29–30)

Although O'Hagan's claim to being "an old horse handler" was certainly legitimate, it wasn't the whole story. Until Gary Geddes's 1977 article "The Writer That CanLit Forgot" was published, the only biographical material a reader would most likely encounter on O'Hagan was that recorded in Harvey Fergusson's introduction to the 1960 edition of *Tay John*, reprinted in 1974, and in the similar jacket copy of the 1958 Doubleday edition of *Wilderness Men*, and in neither case did the writer let on that O'Hagan had even entered public school.

Fergusson, a friend of O'Hagan's and the author of a mountain-man novel called *Wolf Song* (1927),[3] writes in the introduction:

> He was born near the Crow's Nest Pass and grew up north of there on Yellowhead Lake, both in the Canadian Rockies, one of the last great wilderness areas in North America. From an early age he felt the power of the mountains. By the time he was sixteen he was working as an axe-man on survey parties. Later he became a guide and packer for the Fred Brewster Outfit, Jasper, Alberta. In the fall, the summer's routine with horses ended, he travelled the trails alone or with a companion, a pack on his back and a two-and-a-half pound axe his only tool and weapon.

This, of course, is the kind of stuff that sells books. And it is all true, it just leaves rather a lot out. Although critics should be immune to such things, the evocation of a colourful authorial persona does affect a reader's response. Michael Ondaatje entitled his 1974 article on the novel "O'Hagan's Rough-Edged Chronicle"; it is an excellent article — indeed the only one published on *Tay John* for many years, but the title may create a false impression if a reader infers from it that Jackie Denham's description of the typical backwoods tale as a "rough-edged chronicle" can serve as a good description of O'Hagan's novel itself. In *A Reader's Guide to Canadian Literature* (1981), John Moss called O'Hagan a "naïve visionary," and said that "O'Hagan is a creative writer as primitive, or 'natural,' as any published in Canada this century. His unconventional novel reminds one vaguely of a painting on which Marc Chagall and Grandma Moses have collaborated" (221); Moss retained this judgement in the second edition of his guide, which appeared in 1987.

O'Hagan really did pack, survey, and guide in the mountains, but he also received a law degree from McGill University, where he studied under, among others, Stephen Leacock. He was the associate editor of the *McGill Daily* in 1921–22, its editor in chief in 1923–24, and its president in 1924–25. That year, he served as vice president of the Student Council and president of the Literary and Debating Society. Clearly he was not someone who communicated only in grunts, despite his excellent wilderness skills. Further, while he was writing for the *Daily*, so was A.J.M. Smith, a longtime friend and a key figure in the introduction of modernism to Canada. Smith wrote "The Dilettante" column for the *Daily* in 1923–24, and the following year became, of course, a leading light in the production of the *Daily*'s literary supplement. In other words, O'Hagan was ideally located, in Canadian terms, to pick up the latest news of both English and American avant-garde writing.[4] In addition, during the period he was working on *Tay John*, between 1934 and 1939, O'Hagan was living in Berkeley, California, and became closely associated with both the artistic and university communities there. Yet he can almost be blamed for engineering his own misreading.

Again, a comparison with Lowry is instructive. *Under the Volcano* quickly establishes itself as an avant-garde text. Its protagonist, Firmin, struggles with his fall, attempts to write, and sees himself as Dr. Faustus, damned by a too-inquiring intellect. Another character, M. Laruelle, an avant-garde artist, is described as "carrying at the back of his mind the notion of making in France a modern film version of the Faustus story with some such character as Trotsky for its protagonist . . ." (27–28). Firmin and Laruelle clearly belong to the group of intellectuals and artistic producers who, as Bourdieu points out, set themselves up against the bourgeoisie by engaging in "symbolic provocations" (316). Jackie Denham however, seldom speaks of his past, "over which loomed the shadow of a great white house in the north of Ireland, in the county of Tyrone" (75–76). All Lowry's characters plan to return to Europe; Denham is content to drink up his remittance in Edmonton and return to the mountains. Jackie does not write, he speaks, and he speaks not of a lost culture, or of the old days, but of a culture in the making. Lowry peppers his text with the names of writers, musicians, film directors, and artists from the West's classic and avant-garde canons:

How, in a flash, that had brought back the old days of the cinema . . . the days of the Student of Prague, and Wiene and Werner Krauss and Karl Grüne, the Ufa days when a defeated Germany was winning the respect of the cultured world by the pictures she was making. (24)

O'Hagan, on the other hand, buries his allusions to Joseph Conrad, E.M. Forster, and other canonical writers under a naïve, even a vulgar or popular surface. Thus the novel's final image of Tay John towing Ardith Aeriola's body on a toboggan contains not only allusions to the mythic descent of the vegetation deity so popular among modernists such as T.S. Eliot and A.J.M. Smith, but also to a sentimental poem by Duncan Campbell Scott of the sort emphatically rejected by modernists ("On the Way to the Mission"), and, most disturbingly for a Canadian reader, to the doggerel of Robert Service's "The Cremation of Sam McGee," quite firmly rejected by almost everybody, except, of course, the ordinary reader. (The narrator of Service's poem, "horror-driven," hastens through a "land of death" with a corpse "lashed to a sleigh" [63].)

Anyone who does not know O'Hagan's background might feel alarmed by such a grotesque conjunction of clashing allusions, and conclude that O'Hagan was simply unable to control his material. Terry Eagleton argues that

[e]very literary text is built out of a sense of its potential audience, includes an image of whom it is written *for*: every work encodes within itself what Iser calls an "implied reader," intimates in its every gesture the kind of "addressee" it anticipates. (84)

If Eagleton is correct, perhaps we should assume that O'Hagan was ultimately more interested in finding readers in his own mountain territory, in establishing himself as a true mountain man, than in reaching out to an audience that would appreciate the sophistication of his novel.

NOTES

¹ A version of this paper was delivered at the Association for Canadian and Quebec Literatures Conference in Hamilton, Ontario, in May 1987. I thank the ACQL for travel funds. I also thank Brian Trehearne, Department of English, McGill University, for helping me with material on A.J.M. Smith, the *McGill Daily*, and the *McGill Fortnightly Review*.

² For publication information and a description of these three works, see Richard Arnold's "Howard O'Hagan: An Annotated Bibliography," in this volume (Woodcock D12; Ondaatje C9; Atwood C10).

³ Harvey Fergusson's career and writing are described in the biography by Robert Gish, which also contains a photograph of, and a few fleeting references to, O'Hagan.

⁴ Smith's discovery of T.S. Eliot most likely took place in 1924 or 1925, shortly before O'Hagan graduated (Trehearne 337n). Whether Smith and O'Hagan ever discussed Eliot or modernism is not clear. However, they were in touch during O'Hagan's California days; Smith's papers, held by the University of Toronto, contain several manuscripts by O'Hagan, including one with a Berkeley address.

O'Hagan was on the editorial board of the *McGill Daily* when a financial dispute between the editorial board of the *Daily* and Smith and F.R. Scott, editors of the *McGill Daily Literary Supplement*, ended the *Supplement*'s publication run. This rift led to the founding of the *McGill Fortnightly Review* in late 1925 by Smith, Scott, and Leon Edel. Scott and Edel tended to lay the blame for the rift on the insensitivity of an editor of the *Daily*. If that editor was O'Hagan, it seems to have made no difference to the friendship between him and Smith. Edel's versions of the events surrounding the founding of the *McGill Fortnightly Review* can be found in several of his writings: "*The McGill Fortnightly Review*: A Casual Reminiscence," "When McGill Modernized Canadian Literature: Literary Revolution — The 'Montreal Group,' " and "The Young Warrior in the Twenties." In Gary Geddes's "The Writer That CanLit Forgot," O'Hagan tells an anecdote about Smith that may be relevant:

> [Smith] was writing poetry even then [when O'Hagan was on the editorial board of the *Daily*]. I remember him coming in with this poem about a girl's breasts being like ripe plums. "Arthur," I said, "think of the Dean of Women, Miss Hurlbatt. There's no way we can print this." I think he damn near wept. (86)

### WORKS CITED

Black, Paul J. "Malcolm Lowry's *Under the Volcano*: A Critical Reception Study." MA thesis. U of Windsor, 1966.

Bourdieu, Pierre. *Distinction: A Social Critique of the Judgement of Taste*. Trans. Richard Nice. Cambridge: Harvard UP, 1984.

Eagleton, Terry. *Literary Theory: An Introduction*. Minneapolis: U of Minnesota P, 1983.

Edel, Leon. "*The McGill Fortnightly Review*: A Casual Reminiscence." *McGill News* 21.1 (1939): 19+.

———. "When McGill Modernized Canadian Literature: Literary Revolution — The 'Montreal Group.'" *The McGill You Knew: An Anthology of Memories, 1920–1960.* Ed. Edgar Andrew Collard. Don Mills, ON: Longmans, 1975. 112–22.

———. "The Young Warrior in the Twenties." *On F.R. Scott.* Ed. Sandra Djwa and R. St. John Macdonald. Kingston: McGill-Queen's UP, 1983. 6–16.

Fergusson, Harvey. Introduction. *Tay John.* By Howard O'Hagan. 1960. New Canadian Library 105. Toronto: McClelland, 1974. N. pag.

Geddes, Gary. "The Writer That CanLit Forgot." *Saturday Night* Nov. 1977: 84–92.

Gish, Robert. *Frontier's End: The Life and Literature of Harvey Fergusson.* Lincoln: U of Nebraska P, 1988.

Keate, Stuart. "Intruder in the Wilderness." Rev. of *Tay John*, by Howard O'Hagan. *New York Times Book Review* 13 Mar. 1960: 34.

Lowry, Malcolm. *Under the Volcano.* New York: Reynal, 1947.

MacGillivray, J.R. "Letters in Canada: Fiction." *University of Toronto Quarterly* 9 (1939–40): 239.

Moss, John. *A Reader's Guide to Canadian Literature.* Toronto: McClelland, 1981.

Munro, Alice. "Material." *Something I've Been Meaning to Tell You.* Toronto: McGraw-Hill, 1974. 22–44.

New, William H. Introduction. *Malcolm Lowry: A Reference Guide.* A Reference Guide in Literature. By New. Boston: Hall, 1978. ix–xix.

O'Hagan, Howard. Letter to George Woodcock. 1 July 1975. George Woodcock Papers. Queen's University, Kingston.

———. *Tay John.* London: Laidlaw, 1939.

Ohmann, Richard. "The Shaping of a Canon: U.S. Fiction, 1960–75." *Canons.* Ed. Robert von Hallberg. Chicago: U of Chicago P, 1984. 377–401.

Roberts, Kevin. "Talking to Howard O'Hagan." *Event* 5.3 (1976): 41–48.

Robertson, George. "Mountain Man Mythology." Rev. of *Tay John*, by Howard O'Hagan. *Canadian Literature* 9 (1961): 65–66.

Service, Robert. "The Cremation of Sam McGee." *The New Oxford Book of Canadian Poetry in English.* Ed. Margaret Atwood. Toronto: Oxford UP, 1982. 62–64.

Steele, Charles, ed. *Taking Stock: The Calgary Conference on the Canadian Novel.* Proc. of a Conference. 16–18 Feb. 1978. Downsview, ON: ECW, 1982.

Swinnerton, Frank. "New Novels." *Observer* [London] 19 Mar. 1939: 6.

Rev. of *Tay John*, by Howard O'Hagan. *Times Literary Supplement* 18 Mar. 1939: 166.

Rev. of *Tay John*, by Howard O'Hagan. *Canadian Forum* 19 Sept. 1939: 199.

Trehearne, Brian. *Aestheticism and the Canadian Modernists: Aspects of a Poetic Influence*. Kingston: McGill-Queen's UP, 1989.

Watt, F.W. "Letters in Canada: Fiction." Rev. of *Tay John*, by Howard O'Hagan. *University of Toronto Quarterly* 30 (1961): 414–15.

# The Country of Illusion:
# Vision, Change, and Misogyny
# in Howard O'Hagan's *Tay John*

RONALD GRANOFSKY

The mountain country that Howard O'Hagan describes in his 1939 novel, *Tay John*, is one in which vision is unreliable and illusion endemic. Jack Denham, the narrator for much of the novel, urges us to "Remember that I speak to you in the country of illusion, where a chain of mountains in the distance seems no more than a dog might leap across . . ." (163). This mountain country is men's country, a place where the piercing of a mountain range by the laying of railroad tracks is an expression of a driving male urge to create new facts in the material world in the face of temptations to lapse into stasis. Female figures represent the greatest and most dangerous temptation in this country because of their illusory promise of the most desirable of all states of stasis, immortality. In *Tay John*, doubtful vision, stasis and change, and the interaction of men and women are linked not only by means of the incidents of the narrative, but also by a complex structure of images that includes the shadow, the circle, the bear, and the owl. The unknown and the unreal become threats to a male, even Adamic, drive to name, to reify, and to know.

Uncertain vision leads to problems in determining reality. O'Hagan creates a remarkable formal and thematic indeterminacy within a story located specifically, from the opening sentence onward, in historical time and physical space. Uncertainty is generated in the interplay among the mythic, legendary, and realistic sections of the text, and, as Margery Fee has pointed out, in the tension produced by the continually shifting generic ground (14). Paradigmatic of the novel's indeterminacy is the night Tay John spends alone with Julia Alderson. Like E.M. Forster in *A Passage to India* (1924), O'Hagan deliberately obscures the issue here so that it is impossible to tell exactly what happens. Dark nights in the Rockies, like the gloom of the Marabar Caves, render all perception problematic. Is Mrs. Alderson telling the truth when she goads her husband into action by crying, " 'Arthur, Arthur, don't you understand? — Are you blind? — he — he [Tay John] — imposed himself upon me' " (145)? Does she mean what the men believe she means? Is she perhaps mistaken or even maliciously fanciful? Her refusal to make a statement to the Mounties only increases the ambiguity. There is neither evidence nor a finding. Vision has failed.

Far from emulating Conrad's artistic credo, above all to make the reader *see*, then, O'Hagan renders all vision in *Tay John* doubtful, including the reader's: "Do you see?" asks Jack Denham, referring to his first encounter with Tay John. "I was an onlooker. I saw what he didn't see. I saw him, for instance" (79). In one of his philosophical asides, Denham claims that "It is not darkness man fears. It is his helplessness before eyes which see when his own are blinded" (243). So Tay John, whose vision is keener than most, is a man to be feared. The Mountie recruit who accompanies him back from his cabin to face questioning about his night with Mrs. Alderson comments that "the man has eyes . . . eyes, eyes" (151). He is valued as a guide because "His eyes are good" (55). But for Denham, there is a certain security in the knowledge that stasis is inevitable because all perception is unreliable. Alf Dobble, the entrepreneur who is attempting to create a resort in the Rockies, is to be avoided, in Denham's view, because "all men of visions are dangerous to a settled way of life . . ." (173). On the other hand, although Dobble "could not fairly be called blind to facts," his belief, like all beliefs, "is necessarily a form of intellectual myopia" (225). Dobble is finally defeated by the mountains he is attempting to remake according to his vision of the future, but Denham's verdict on the man is equivocal. Although a myopic visionary at best, Dobble "must be given credit for the courage of his illusions" (164). Furthermore, he does effect one permanent change in naming the place of his defeat Lucerne.

Vision is so problematic in this borderland country because different versions of time are operative in the various worlds adjacent to it and among the various inhabitants. The issue of time (as well as place) enters the novel in its very first sentence: "The time of this in its beginning, in men's time, is 1880 in the summer, and its place is the Athabaska valley . . ." (11). Arnold E. Davidson labels the two concepts of time in the novel "chronological, historical, on the one hand; and, on the other, timeless legend verging toward timelessness" (36). But the opening sentence speaks of "men's time" rather than "man's time." In fact, with the opposition between a vertical and a horizontal temporality, there seems to be a close association between the conflict of men and women in *Tay John*, and differing concepts of time also inherent in the relations between the Indians and white settlers. Standing ambiguously between the two are Tay John and his Nick Carraway-like admirer, Jack Denham.

Vision and temporal change coincide in the story of Tay John's putative father, Red Rorty, whose importance to the Shuswap people is based on the claim "that he could see to-morrow" (30). That tomorrow promises a leader of true vision, one who would be able to perceive things others could not. They had been led into their present state of affairs, they believe, by "a bad leader" (30), one who could not accurately anticipate the extrapolation into the future of present conditions. Even before he is born, then, Tay John is fixed in a role requiring a special kind of perception. From the first, he is associated with the shadow motif, an apt symbol of ambiguous vision. The interaction of the concept of problematic perception with the shadow motif may well derive from Plato's allegory of the cave, which Fee has related to O'Hagan's novel (11–12). In that allegory, of course, men take the shadows that they can see for the substance that they cannot. O'Hagan's mountain country becomes, in this context, a microcosm of a universal human inability to distinguish illusion from reality.

The vertically thrusting mountains are the most obvious image in *Tay John* of a stasis that challenges man's ability to alter the existing environment; the railroad cutting across them horizontally is the most prominent image of man-made change. But the issue of change and stasis is complicated by the paradox, best articulated by Susanne Langer, that although "[p]ermanence of form . . . is the constant aim of living matter," permanence of form itself is *a pattern of changes* (66). Every living organism seeks to maintain itself intact, but that goal can be accomplished only by a constant renewal, as in the absorption of other living forms through ingestion. O'Hagan does not seem to favour either stasis or change per se; he records their conflict.

Red Rorty resists change, perhaps because he lives on the edge of it: "In 1880 one man remained by the Athabaska river where it flowed through the mountains" (13). Red Rorty's isolation makes his vision suspect: "he was given to hearing strange sounds and to seeing a tree far off as a man, or a bunch of trees down the valley from his cabin as a group of men advancing towards him" (14).

Red Rorty lives in a spatial borderland between two geographical worlds, and in a temporal borderland, when those worlds are about to be united by the work of men. His dramatic change in life is a rejection of the flesh for the spirit. Stopping one day at the church instead of continuing, as was his wont, "to the houses in the east-end of town where the women waited" (15), he becomes a preacher of "The Way." As he moves from one side of the divide to the other, Rorty sets fire to nearly all his worldly possessions, saying, "These things that I burn are for to-day. I live for tomorrow and for the days that come after" (19). His later backsliding from the world of the spirit to that of the flesh is also accompanied by fire. When he finds sexual ease with a married woman of the Shuswap tribe, among whom he has gone to preach the gospel, he is chased into the wood by the women, tied to a tree, and set on fire. Fire is the symbolic element of change in the novel, while stasis is suggested by water (the elemental opposite of fire) in the form of snow, which can "cover, as if for ever, the landscape" (92).

Alf Dobble also lives for tomorrow and the days that come after. Like Red Rorty's change, Dobble's is within tightly controlled limits. Both believe in a pattern that is perceivable only to the true believer: Rorty in a confused evangelical Christianity and Dobble in the coming of tourism. They believe in a predetermined future. By way of contrast, Jack Denham is described as "a man whose pride was in his past" (75). Red's change intersects with the communal yearning for change of the Shuswap, itself a result of the deteriorating conditions of life imposed upon them by the ongoing change produced by the inexorably migrating whites. The Shuswap Indians wish to end their long separation from the Salish tribes along the coast by crossing the mountains behind a leader not yet born. Red Rorty's evangelism seems to fit in well with their Messianic mythology.

But the Shuswap, settled for so long in one place, are, in fact, associated most strongly not with the horizontal but with the vertical dimension of life, an association imagistically suggested in their winter-time custom of going "underground for the warmth, digging great holes and supporting the sides with poles from the forest" (22), and rising "up from their houses through the snow in the morning like bodies from the grave . . ." (31). Their collective wish to be reunited with their cousins is a wish for a circular return to origins far different from the

European settlers' crossing of the mountains to what, for them, is new land. Red Rorty's vision and theirs do not really coincide, and his death at their hands after he has transgressed one of their laws makes this clear. In place of the booming word that promised them change, a stone, like the stone mountains themselves, a symbol of stasis, is put between the jaws of Red Rorty.[1]

The Shuswap faith is both "the substance of things hoped for," and "the shadow of what they could not yet discern" (29). As the embodiment of the Shuswap faith, Tay John, too, must be both substance and shadow. That he at first lacks a shadow, and, even after attaining one, has only precarious possession of it, anticipates the resistance he is to show throughout his life to fulfilling the expectations of others. Fee makes an analogous point in terms of the continual replacement of one genre by another in the novel: "Tay John . . . will not stay put. He moves from myth to epic romance, to realism; escapes irony by moving into comedy, and finally moves into myth again" (14). Tay John also moves or threatens movement in a more literal sense. Significantly, it is a wise old woman who finds a shadow for Tay John, an action that ensures his continued presence among the Shuswap.

The shadow is a complex symbol in *Tay John*. Suggestive at once of presence and absence, it is also a reminder in the daylight world of the darkness of night, and, because it is featureless, it emphasizes the border between those two worlds. Whatever the shadow may suggest in any particular context, it is clearly aligned with the forces of determinism and stasis, as the remarkable opening pages of part 3 serve to indicate. Tay John "looked for the new," we are told there, but "there is nothing new." This is so because the present "was implicit in time's beginning." And although we may "walk upon the earth in light," at the core of that light, "imprisoned in its fires," is the "first vast and awful darkness" to which we must inevitably return. The shadow is the reminder of our fate, "the day's memories of the night." Each man's shadow "is his shroud, awaiting him by his mother's womb," a reminder of what he knew until the moment of birth, that "we are returning. We have made the circle" (161–62). What is interesting in these pages is the alignment of woman with the images of stagnation and death: darkness, shadow, and the circle. However, we must remember that these are the thoughts of Jack Denham, a narrator as unreliable as Fitzgerald's Nick Carraway. Denham's attitude toward change and stasis is highly ambivalent.

Throughout the novel, Tay John poses a potentially anarchic threat to a static or predetermined set of circumstances. He aligns himself, whenever possible, with the forces of change, but is in continual danger of falling into stasis. Like Joe Christmas in Faulkner's *Light in August* (1932), Tay John belongs completely to neither of the two races from which he derives, and so represents in his very appearance the anarchic threat of miscegenation. But O'Hagan's novel is not so much concerned with race itself as it is with the epistemological issues that lie behind its perception, and the horizontal and vertical axes with which the races are associated.

Tay John is forever caught between the need for an individual completion that includes the sexual imperative, and a desire to evade all fates including his own and the one he shares with all mortals, most frequently represented in the novel by the circle. At the beginning of Tay John's life, change seems to require a break with woman. When first discovered by the Shuswap tribe, Kumkleseem, as Tay John is originally known among his people, dwells in the borderland between life and death. Persephone-like, he seems to spend part of his day underground at his mother's grave and part of it above ground. He is lured to the Indian village by the planting of 12 bows at spaced intervals. Describing a partial circle, the bow suggests a lack of completion, which, in some way, is also indicated by the missing shadow. His tribe's refusal to sanction Tay John's sexual demands when he reaches manhood is an attempt to create an unbreakable link between his individual fate and their communal fate. States one of the tribe elders: "The woman of Tay John is the people. He is a leader of the people and is married to their sorrows" (67). His departure is at one and the same time an assertion of individual priorities over communal ones and a rejection of determinism itself. Connected to all of Tay John's triumphs and failures are female figures.

Tay John both resists and is attracted to woman and what she represents. At times, he will stand for long moments in front of a picture hanging in McLeod's cabin, "a large print of a girl, veiled in mists of modesty, who was *always* about to step into a fresh and bubbling pool, by whose sides the grass was *forever* green, the trees *eternally* in leaf, and the sky *steadfastly* blue" (96; emphasis added). Opposed conceptually to this state of permanence is the world and time of men, specifically the men who are blazing trails, moving forward in the wilderness, piercing the mountains in order to forge a horizontal link across the country: "Still, on that survey we were aware of time. We worked feverishly, sixteen hours a day when the days were long" (91). The very independence of Canada as a country is linked to the creation of the railroad, albeit in something of a cart-before-the-horse manner:

> So that it might be built and that men might gain money from its building, Canada was made a dominion. British Columbia, a colony of England, became the most western province of the territory now stretching from the Atlantic to the Pacific. (11)

Similarly, only by resisting the timeless "female" world can a man apparently assure himself of his independence.

In the world of *Tay John*, women are dangerous. Julia Alderson's perfume reminds McLeod "of the beaver castor men rub upon their traps" (120). But they are also portrayed as disgusting, at least to some men. Ardith Aeriola "draws men like a piece of bad meat draws flies" (252), according to Jay Wiggins, a Mounted Police inspector. The misogyny of the novel is a function of the taming of the natural world; as in Faulkner, it is a result of the confrontation with the unknown wilderness: "A new mountain valley leads a man on like that — like a woman he has never touched" (80). Vision plays an important part in the struggle with the unknown: "It is only your vision that holds it [a new mountain valley] in the known and created world" (80). In *The Lay of the Land*, Annette Kolodny speculates that "gendering the land as feminine" bespeaks "a *need* to experience the land as a nurturing, giving maternal breast because of the threatening, alien, and potentially emasculating terror of the unknown" (8–9). In such a situation, men's fears become projected all too easily upon actual women.

The attitude toward women in *Tay John* is not as purely negative as it is in other mountain-man novels, where, according to David Stouck, "there is a deep strain of misogyny" (217). Stouck cites A.B. Guthrie Jr.'s *The Big Sky* (1947), in which "there is overt and glaring misogyny in even the smallest details of the novel, such as Dick's passing recollection of the starving men who found two Indian women, raped them, and then ate them" (217). In his 1977 novel *The School-Marm Tree*, in fact, O'Hagan uses a female protagonist. Selva's aspirations in that novel shed some light upon what O'Hagan is concerned about in *Tay John*. In 1925, Selva dreams of leaving her stultifying home in the foothills town of Yellowhead, a divisional point for the railroad. Her dreams become embodied in Peter Wrogg, a British visitor to the town, who vaguely holds out the promise of a life for Selva back East, in Montreal: "He was the shape and substance of dream, the lustre of her hopes, an emissary from that world where she wished to be. As such, she had created him, fashioned him from loneliness and hunger . . ." (196). There are images of symbolic castration in the novel. Peter has his tongue nearly severed in a fight; Selva encounters a man who has lost both legs in a train accident. That Peter is defeated by the mountains — killed, in fact — represents not the defeat of the man but the defeat, to paraphrase D.H. Lawrence, of the woman who would have ridden away from Yellowhead. As Peter prepares to depart on his fateful journey, Selva has these thoughts about the proper role of men and women: "Early man had been a hunter. To hunt he had to travel. His woman stayed at home. This morning she too would stay at home" (220).

In 1974, O'Hagan responded to a question about the difference between men and women: "Ah it's the same as their sexual makeup. A man looks outward because his genitals are on the outside. A woman looks inside because she's built that way" (Roberts 45). While it is arguable that in a frontier society the majority of men will tend to be trapped in a simplistic view of the sexes, it is reductive in the extreme to maintain that men and women are so conditioned by the facts of their anatomy that they will think, act, and react in predetermined ways, and that all sense of individual differences will be eclipsed. In fact, in *Tay John*, O'Hagan is doing decidedly more than simply equating movement with the male and stasis with the female, although he is undeniably doing that as well. He is also using the concept of unreliable vision and endemic illusion to throw into question any easy value judgements that we may be tempted to ascribe to each, a temptation he himself evidently succumbed to in later years.

"Your Westerner," Jack Denham tells us helpfully, is not only one born "blind . . . dropped by his mother upon the ground, but also one who came with his eyes open" (162). Such a man is engaged in a paradoxical quest for change and death at the same time: "Give us new earth, we cry; new places, that we may see our shadows shaped in forms that man has never seen before" (162–63). It is a quest for the obliteration of time as a continuum, its transformation into a timeless Now that ultimately means stasis rather than immortality. It is a kind of blindness: "Let us go on so quickly that we see the future as the past" (163). Various incidents in *Tay John* illustrate the complex interplay among vision, change, and woman that is at the heart of O'Hagan's fictional exploration.

In the Shuswap world, loss of a certain kind of vision is related to the adult, the communal, and the female. In their wisdom, the Shuswap people realize that a period of separation is a necessary prelude to a true feeling of community, but the initiation can be successful only if a new kind of vision replaces the old. When a boy approaches manhood, he is expected to isolate himself from the tribe until visited by a fast-induced vision. The child lives "in a land of his own creating" from which the adults are barred, since their eyes "no longer saw the visions of his eyes" (44).

When Tay John reaches the edge of manhood, his people await a transformation that will make him conscious of his communal responsibilities: "The boy says 'I.' The man says 'We.' . . ." (44). But Tay John resists; like some New World Wordsworth, he wishes to retain the penetrating vision of childhood. Finally conforming to custom, however, he leaves the tribe for the wilderness. Coming to the head of a river after four days, Kumkleseem decides to go no further. The imagery he later chooses to describe his decision is telling. He speaks of the source of the river as a place where a man could step across, but the icy rock walls, "cold as an old woman's breast," convince him that he "had come to the end of [his] journey" (48). This is a place where, Tay John could see, a cow moose had lain three days earlier and a she-bear had crossed. This is woman territory. At night, "an owl, the soul of a departed woman, was in the tree above me, and my ears, become lonely, were tender to its message" (49). He does not cross the boundary, but what he brings home with him is a harbinger of the change about to overtake him and his tribe. He brings back with him a strange, heavy, and dark sand from the bank of the river. It is gold ore. Because of it, Kumkleseem becomes Tay John, more and more a stranger to his own people, who patiently wait, "blind in time" (57).

The bear and the owl are to recur in the novel, and when they do, they are associated with woman and with stasis. In "Jackie's tale," Denham relates how he came across Tay John one day on the far side of a river. The colour white is associated with the stream here (as it is later to be associated with Julia Alderson): "There were rapids. That creek — it was white. It was jagged. It had teeth in it. I felt it would have cut me in two" (78). The episode itself, the archetypal battle between the she-bear and Tay John,[2] makes Denham think of a shadow:

"It was the stuff of a nightmare come alive in broad daylight and throwing its shadow on the ground before you" (78–79). Tay John has finally crossed a boundary, threatening change. Denham's presence on the other side of the carnivorous stream serves to underscore Tay John's transgression.

This is the scene where Denham claims, "I saw what he [Tay John] didn't see. I saw him, for instance" (79). The reader, in turn, patently sees more than Denham, who requires mechanical aid for his vision: "I had my glasses with me, so that I could have a good look at the high country . . ." (79). Moreover, as Denham tells us, Tay John sees the bear long before Denham himself does. The teeth of the river and the "sharp white teeth" of the she-bear reveal to us Denham's fear of being swallowed by woman (86). When he returns to camp, "It was dark, black as the inside of a bear. Night was about me like a covering from which I tried to escape" (90). It should be emphasized that Denham is not opposed to stasis. On the contrary, although he admires Tay John's ability to face change, his own fear holds him back in the known world. The river and woman, both of whom he dreads, separate him from Tay John, the man he would be but cannot reach.

Female figures continue to be associated with Tay John, as Denham relates the story, invariably to his disadvantage. At McLeod's, Tay John meets a man named Timberlake whose vision is imperfect, for "a long time ago he lost an eye" (102). Timberlake owns a sorrel mare with "clean legs" and "a deep chest" (103). As he views her with "her haunch touched and her flank shadowed by the fading sunlight" (103), Tay John feels he must have her for "she would raise him above the ground and his feet would no longer be the servants of rocky trails" (103). As McLeod supposes, Tay John sees the mare "as more than a horse" (103).

In his essay entitled "The Fear of Women in Prairie Fiction: An Erotics of Space," Robert Kroetsch refers to "Horse:house" as an important "grammatical pair" in Prairie fiction:

> To be *on* a horse is to move: motion into distance. To be *in* a house is to be fixed: a centering unto stasis. Horse is masculine. House is feminine. Horse:house. Masculine:feminine. On:in. Motion: stasis. A woman ain't supposed to move. (76)

That Tay John's horse is a mare complicates the equation, of course. She is also described as half in the light and half in shadow. Though

Red Rorty might have subscribed to Kroetsch's "resolution of the dialectic" of horse:house in "whore's-house" (76), clearly for Tay John, with the sorrel mare representing both horse and female, there is no resolution.

That Tay John is badly mistaken in his view of the mare is suggested not only by the subsequent events involving the mare herself, but also by what he must do in order to gain possession of her. McLeod suggests that Timberlake and Tay John cut a pack of cards with Timberlake's horse and Tay John's furs as stakes. The scene is set by McLeod's fire: "New shadows danced in the room, and for a time the lantern hanging above was dimmed in the blaze from the chimney corner" (106). The fire symbolically suggests Tay John's attempts to change his way of life; the shadow suggests the forces ranged against him. Tay John cuts first, and turns up the (one-eyed) jack of spades. He likes his chances. Denham's juxtaposition of vision, horse, and woman in his Conradian or, rather, Marlovian description of the incident is telling: "His horse, on which he would ride to his destiny like a warrior to the wars. In the dim light I dare say he could see the picture of that white-skinned girl above the head of McLeod's bed" (106). Timberlake cuts and turns up the (two-eyed) queen of hearts: "He had won by one card. He had the white-skinned woman on his side" (107). Tay John then severs his own left hand, still clutching the card, with an axe.

Timberlake relinquishes the mare out of sheer amazement, but the symbolic pattern is clear. Tay John's defeat is connected with those who normally have poorer vision than he does, with a shadowy scene and female figures. His own blind faith in chance has issued in a determined result; his attempts to change in stasis. His self-mutilation is, on this level of significance, a self-castration. The phallic, searching, moving male wins his point only at the cost of his very manhood because he has miscalculated the odds. Tay John's quoting scripture as he swings the axe evokes the memory of Red Rorty and his fate at the hands of women. His defeat, moreover, is decidedly within the vertical dimension: "Tay John was back on the ground again" (107). He resists the force of determinism, however, even as his actions conform to it symbolically, for, now possessing only one hand, Tay John adopts his second new identity: "Now I am no longer Tay John. Now they will call me The One-Handed" (110).

Tay John loses the mare eventually. She will not be subjugated to the man, and is, moreover, community-minded: "a horse alone needs the herd" (115). He replaces her with a gelding. Yet, it is the mare who leads Tay John across the river, to the low country, "where men under canvas sought a way for the rails into the mountains" (113). But the white way of transgression is not quite Tay John's; he dwells in the borderland between worlds: "He was a man who had left the world he knew, the world of his own people, and moved now on the rim of the white man's world forming around him" (99).

The dominating female figure in the third part of the novel, Ardith Aeriola, is described by Denham in generic terms: "Here was woman. Here was man's promise of immortality. Here was man's ease, and here, too, his torment" (199). Ardith attracts not only Tay John but also Alf Dobble and Red Rorty's younger brother, the priest, Thomas, whose story clearly links vision, change, and woman.

Unlike his brother, Father Rorty has a hushed voice that seldom rises above a whisper. But he, too, seeks a clearer vision of life. A lock of his hair frequently falls over his eyes, and he habitually brushes it aside "as if he strove to clear an image from before his fine, blue eyes better to see the world" (183). In the mountain camps where he plies his trade, Father Rorty's enemy is woman, particularly the mountain prostitutes who occasionally appear on the scene. The conflict between spirit and flesh is starkly set up, and it will be internalized within the priest once Ardith arrives. Her arrival reminds Denham "that woman was the death of heroes and the destruction of heroes' work — but heroes, those vulnerable men, are gone from the earth, and woman's power therefore no longer what once it was" (192).

Ardith arouses in Thomas Rorty the dormant realization that even for him change is possible, albeit at the price of transgression. She precipitates in him a crisis of faith, which leads him to a self-imposed trial that ends in death. In his letter to Ardith, found by Denham, Father Rorty quotes from St. Augustine's *Confessions*: "the flesh lusteth against the spirit, and the spirit against the flesh" (211). At times, he imagines that he will cross the lake separating Ardith's tent from the main camp, "and come out before your tent, a man" (213). But, like Denham, Father Rorty fails to cross a demarcating body of water; he remains a prisoner of his old way of thinking. In emulation of Christ, he ties himself to a "school-marm tree" and becomes trapped (217). Self-crucified, as his brother was crucified by others, he dies of exposure.

In his later novel *The School-Marm Tree*, O'Hagan describes such a tree as follows:

It was a pine tree whose upper trunk had been broken off by the wind. Two great branches had grown up to usurp the place of the trunk so that the tree now resembled a gigantic human figure . . . enfolding the wind in its arms. (54)

As the name suggests, the human figure is female. Viewing the school-marm tree after Rorty's death, Denham finds that "It stood sturdy, rather than tall, stark and black against the sunset. To me in those moments it had no phallic form" (217). But if woman is the immediate cause of Thomas Rorty's death, and shadow is imagistically associated with it (219–20), the two directions of the cross, the vertical and the horizontal, clearly representing spirit and flesh here, image the structural pattern of conflict evident throughout the novel. Woman is the priest's enemy not so much because she represents the flesh and he the spirit, as that she represents a rival for the vertical direction of man's soul out of time. Father Rorty, in the mind of Denham, at least, thought to himself, "I will lift myself higher than any man before me, except Christ Himself, has been lifted" (219). In the end, he is "impaled upon the tree like time upon the hour" (220). As Ardith does later, Thomas Rorty dies with his mouth filled with snow (220, 262), a symbol of the illusion of permanence that is explicitly associated with woman elsewhere: "In the winter silence was about them on the snow like a name each had heard whispered in his mother's womb" (75). His death makes others doubt their perception. Alf Dobble remarks, "It is unbelievable. I doubt my eyes" (221).

In many ways, Ardith seems an apt mate for Tay John. Like him, she lives for the present; like him, she takes on an assumed name. They are both people of border country (in Denham's estimation): "Each of them, Ardith and Tay John, in manners distinct, stalked the boundaries of society without every [sic] fully entering" (252–53). She is connected to the railroad and so to the horizontal direction. But, clearly, Ardith represents a danger as well. Unlike Julia Alderson, who is consistently associated with white, Ardith is dark:

She had black hair. A small face. Her eyes were dark. And when I say dark, I don't mean simply brown. They were black, so black that by comparison their whites showed slightly blue — fragile, clear as porcelain, so that you felt with a strong light behind her you might through them see the shadow of her being. (198)

Shadow and substance: here Plato's allegory is reversed. Ardith is all substance, no shadow, much like Tay John when he first enters the world.

In a way, Ardith Aeriola is a parody of Tay John. Her very name, suggestive of the air (Latin 'aerius'), counterposes his chthonic origins. Her playful struggles with a declawed bear club parody his life-and-death struggle with the she-grizzly. The little male bear has scratched her, so she has had its nails cut off to the quick. There is an imagistic refrain here of Tay John's self-mutilation, as Michael Ondaatje notes (26), and the fact that the cub has been taken from its mother and given to Ardith suggests Tay John's origins, as well. It seems, then, that both the cub and Ardith herself represent, in ironic form, aspects of Tay John. Her naïve and playful attitude toward the natural world contrasts sharply with Tay John's respectful attitude. Ardith tires of the cub, and asks Tay John to return it to its mother. This is impossible, of course, and Tay John kills it as mercifully as possible. The killing suggests that self-destruction of some sort awaits Tay John in his liaison with Ardith. On the other hand, in his abandonment of his people, Tay John, it could be argued, is the male mountain-whore equivalent of Ardith Aeriola, selling his birthright for a rifle and a red coat, the gifts and trinkets of the white-man's world.

Both Margery Fee and Leslie Monkman view the relationship between Tay John and Ardith positively. Fee writes that "male and female meet and complement each other . . . in the characters of Tay John and Ardith Aeriola" (23), while Monkman contends that the love between them is a fulfilment for both. He implies that it resolves "some of the myriad dualities of red and white, darkness and light, the ideal and the real, divinity and humanity, and love and death" (47). I would contend that the relationship between Tay John and Ardith Aeriola represents the illusion generated by faulty vision. Like the earlier incident with Julia Alderson, its outcome is never clear. The story of their end (on which interpretations of the value of the relationship largely depend) is conveyed to the reader third hand, through the trapper Blackie (who is apparently the last person to see them), through Denham, and through the anonymous narrator. Moreover, the scene takes place in a blizzard: "the snow flew so fast and thick that Blackie when he looked around couldn't see the trees along the shore nor beyond them the mountains" (260). Tay John appears "shadowy like" (260), and seems "like he was to fall" (261). Tay John tries to prevent Blackie from seeing what it is he is lugging on the toboggan, but when they part, Blackie can see that it is a dead woman. Tay John is looking for a church, and Blackie comments, "The man was so done in he was havin' visions — or else he was just plain crazy. A church! . . . An' we couldn't even see the mountain, with the snow and the wind howlin" (261).

The next day, Blackie sets off to find Tay John, but can find only his quickly fading tracks in the snow:

> He followed the trail in and out among the trees. It made in one place a wide circle and returned to within a hundred yards of where it had been before. "The man was all in," Blackie said; "he didn't know where he was goin'. He stumbled. I saw where he fell, and had to pull himself up by the branches of a tree." (263)

The circle, the snow, a dead woman, the rising up with the help of a tree are images whose full significance is dependent upon an accumulation of events and descriptions from earlier in the novel. Blackie finally gives up trying to find Tay John. He has the feeling, though, that "Tay John hadn't gone over the pass at all. He had just walked down, the toboggan behind him, under the snow and into the ground" (264).

This, it must be remembered is Blackie's impression only. He has no facts to base it on. It is an impression formed on a day when vision is suspect and in a world where perception is problematic and illusion rampant. When he arrives in town, Blackie "took from their case a pair of gold-rimmed spectacles as if fearful that his eyes alone could not be trusted to deliver a faithful report of what they saw about him" (259–60). Once again, a key scene is rendered indeterminate by the problematic nature of vision itself.

Blackie's report, of course, is no more unreliable than most of *Tay John*, which is legend or hearsay. The very fact that he had that particular impression, and that the novel ends with it, gives the impression a certain weight in our interpretation of the novel. It suggests that Tay John is the immortal hero of myth, and, as Ondaatje has noted, it implies the completion of a pattern (27). Tay John's beginning and end are similar or inverse versions of each other: he rises at birth from the grave of a woman dead in pregnancy, and descends into death with a woman dead in pregnancy. But it is precisely against pattern, death, and determinism that Tay John has struggled all along. On the realistic level, the love of Tay John and Ardith Aeriola proves mutually destructive, as Fee admits: "His love for Aeriola kills him, as her love for him, her pregnancy, has presumably killed her" (25). Ardith becomes a burden to Tay John, which lessens his chances of survival in a harsh environment. His sexual potency, which represents a challenge to the female principle as presented in the novel, has "killed" her.

Throughout the novel, shadow and circle imagery has kept the concept of determinism in the reader's mind. Now the events at the end of the narrative, which take it full circle to the beginning in a way Fee labels "mythically irresistible" (16), underscore the deterministic pattern to which Tay John finally succumbs after much struggle. While it is true, then, that, as Jack Robinson puts it, "the novel tends to disperse rather than to construct meaning" (95), it is also clear that the novel's protagonist desperately resists meaningful patterns because they represent constriction and, ultimately, death. From the first, however, Tay John's quest for freedom has been tinged with irony. Fleeing his responsibility to lead his people over the mountains, he participates in the struggle to pierce those same mountains for the railroad. He becomes a guide, taking others where they have never been before, but himself repeating the same pattern time after time. Though his vision is excellent, he appears at times to be blind to reality: in the card game with Timberlake, in the blizzard. Tay John's strength, like that of the blinded Samson, is undermined by woman.

There most certainly is misogyny in the novel. But one can reasonably ask whether the misogyny is authorial or ascribed to characters within the text from whom the author distances himself, characters such as McLeod, Denham, and Wiggins. The overwhelming sense of woman as fatal temptress, all the more dangerous because she seems to offer immortality, suggests that the former is true. The obvious and deliberate unreliability of the woman-hating Jack Denham, his cloudy past, his alignment with stasis, and his hero worship of Tay John tend to suggest that the latter is the case.

The portrayal of a forward-looking male drive interacting with a passive, stagnant female inertia at a specific time in Canadian history is qualified and undermined at crucial points in the novel. Tay John is most emphatically *not* trapped by his anatomy or anything else for very long. One-handed, he is as able as any two-handed mountain guide. He quite literally single-handedly defeats the men and forces arrayed against him until his last, ambiguous battle in the snowstorm raises the question of whether he is finally defeated by woman, or united with her in returning to a legendary and timeless world where death is powerless. Vision, change, and the portrayal of woman are all equivocal in *Tay John*, and render the significance of the novel indeterminate. In the end, the unreliability of perception in this country of illusion makes the task of judging what is real and what is true impossible.

NOTES

[1] Arnold E. Davidson makes a similar point regarding the stone: "moreover, with that stone, Red Rorty's mission to eternity ends in stasis and parodic death" (36). Jack Robinson, on the other hand, views the stone in Red Rorty's mouth as symbolic of mendacity (96), an idea that is perhaps better applied to a stone similarly placed in the mouth of the dead Boy Staunton in *Fifth Business*, the first novel of Robertson Davies's Deptford trilogy.

[2] Tay John's struggle with the bear may owe something to Faulkner's story "The Bear," which appeared in its earliest version as "Lion" in *Harper's* in December of 1935. As I have pointed out, there are other affinities with Faulkner evident in the novel.


WORKS CITED

Davidson, Arnold E. "Silencing the Word in Howard O'Hagan's *Tay John*." *Canadian Literature* 110 (1986): 30–44.

Fee, Margery. "Howard O'Hagan's *Tay John*: Making New World Myth." *Canadian Literature* 110 (1986): 8–27.

Kolodny, Annette. *The Lay of the Land: Metaphor as Experience and History in American Life and Letters*. Chapel Hill: U of Carolina P, 1975.

Kroetsch, Robert. "The Fear of Women in Prairie Fiction: An Erotics of Space." *Crossing Frontiers: Papers in American and Canadian Western Literature*. Ed. Dick Harrison. Proc. of a Conference. 12–15 April 1978. Edmonton: U of Alberta P, 1979: 73–83.

Langer, Susanne K. *Feeling and Form: A Theory of Art Developed from "Philosophy in a New Key."* New York: Scribner's, 1953.

Monkman, Leslie. *A Native Heritage: Images of the Indian in English-Canadian Literature*. Toronto: U of Toronto P, 1981.

O'Hagan, Howard. *The School-Marm Tree*. Vancouver: Talonbooks, 1977.

——. *Tay John*. 1960. New Canadian Library 105. Toronto: McClelland, 1974.

Ondaatje, Michael. "O'Hagan's Rough-Edged Chronicle." *Canadian Literature* 61 (1974): 24–31.

Roberts, Kevin. "Talking to Howard O'Hagan." *Event* 5.3 (1976): 41–48.

Robinson, Jack. "Dismantling Sexual Dualities: O'Hagan's *Tay John*." *Alberta: Studies in the Arts and Sciences* 2.2 (1990): 93–108.

Stouck, David. "The Art of the Mountain Man Novel." *Western American Literature* 20 (1985): 211–22.

# Howard O'Hagan:
# An Annotated Bibliography

RICHARD ARNOLD

Some items that those familiar with O'Hagan's writings might expect to find in this bibliography have not been listed. There are several reasons for this. O'Hagan's contributions to the *McGill Daily*, for example, were not given a byline. Similarly, much of his early journalism remained anonymous. Some items mentioned in interviews and letters as having been published in certain periodicals simply could not be found. For example, "The Woman Who Got On at Jasper Station" (or "The Woman Who Got On at Sacramento," as is the title in some references) is mentioned a number of times as having been published in *Esquire*; however, it is not listed in the index to this magazine, nor did a search of the periodical itself turn it up. On the verso of the title page of the first edition of *Wilderness Men* are listed acknowledgements of the previous publication of four stories: "The Beast," "The Trapper of Rat River," "The Warpath of Almighty Voice," and "The Bloody Ordeal of Trapper John." Only two of these titles (the second and third) can be traced. Careful checking of *Argosy* and *True*, the most likely publishers of "The Beast" and "The Bloody Ordeal of Trapper John" respectively, turned up nothing. Other Popular and Fawcett publications have been checked to no avail. It is possible that O'Hagan was paid for these stories but that they were never published, as sometimes happens. Further, we have anecdotal evidence of more radio productions of O'Hagan's work. However, the CBC Archives does not have a comprehensive catalogue, and so not every production that we heard of could be checked. Finally, although nonsequential page references for popular magazines are normally indicated by a plus sign after the first page reference, we have included all page references; since so few libraries hold the popular magazines O'Hagan wrote for, this practice facilitates interlibrary loan requests.

# BIBLIOGRAPHY
## *Table of Contents*

## Part I WORKS BY HOWARD O'HAGAN

## A Books (Novels, Short Stories and Sketches), and Manuscripts

### Novels

A1  *Tay John.* London: Laidlaw, 1939. 263 pp.
*Tay John.* 2nd ed. Introd. Harvey Fergusson. New York: Clarkson N. Potter, 1960. 263 pp.
*Tay John.* 1960. Introd. Patricia Morley. New Canadian Library 105. Toronto: McClelland, 1974. 263 pp.
*Tay John.* 1960. Afterword Michael Ondaatje. New Canadian Library 105. Toronto: McClelland, 1989. 272 pp.

A2  *The School-Marm Tree.* Introd. P.K. Page. Vancouver: Talonbooks, 1977. 245 pp.

### Short Stories and Sketches

A3  *Wilderness Men.* Garden City, NY: Doubleday, 1958. 263 pp.
    Includes "The Black Ghost," "The Singer in the Willows," "The Man Who Chose to Die," "The Man Who Walked Naked across Montana," "Grey Owl," "The Little Bear That Climbs Trees," "Montana Pete Goes Courting," " 'The Grass Man' and Walker among Trees," "Shwat — The End of Tzouhalem," and "I Look Upward and See the Mountain against the Sky."
*Wilderness Men.* 2nd ed. Vancouver: Talonbooks, 1978. 189 pp.
    Includes all the stories in the first edition except "Montana Pete Goes Courting."

A4  *The Woman Who Got On at Jasper Station, and Other Stories.* [Denver]: Swallow, 1963. 112 pp.
    Includes "The Woman Who Got On at Jasper Station," "Trees Are Lonely Company," "Ito Fujika, the Trapper," "The Warning," "The Love Story of Mr. Alfred Wimple," "The School-Marm Tree," "The White Horse," and "The Tepee."
*The Woman Who Got On at Jasper Station, and Other Stories.* 2nd ed. Vancouver: Talonbooks, 1977. 132 pp.
    Includes all the stories in the first edition, except for "The School-Marm Tree," which O'Hagan had expanded into the novel of the same

title. This edition has four new stories: "The Stranger," "The Bride's Crossing," "A Mountain Journey," and "The Promised Land."

## Manuscripts

A5    The Howard O'Hagan Papers
       Special Collections
       McPherson Library
       University of Victoria
       PO Box 3045
       Victoria, British Columbia
       V8W 3P4

The University of Victoria Library is the major repository of Howard O'Hagan's manuscripts. The material is housed in seven boxes; an outline of their contents follows.

*Box 1:* Correspondence — personal and business
*Box 2:* Unpublished sections of autobiography; unpublished novel "The Blue Distance"; synopsis of unpublished novel "The Promised Land"
*Box 3:* Drafts of published and unpublished stories and articles
*Box 4:* Manuscripts of *The School-Marm Tree*
*Box 5:* Published stories and articles
*Box 6:* Photographs, articles about O'Hagan, ephemera
*Box 7:* Letters about O'Hagan written by a number of his friends and associates (including his fraternity brothers) to Chris Petter and Margery Fee

A6    Talonbooks Archives
       Special Collections
       W.A.C. Bennett Library
       Simon Fraser University
       Burnaby, British Columbia
       V5A 1S6

Editorial materials and cover art for *The Woman Who Got On at Jasper Station and Other Stories* (1977), *The School-Marm Tree* (1977), and *Wilderness Men* (1978). A letter from O'Hagan to P.K. Page concerning the introduction to *The School-Marm Tree*. Photocopies of the manuscript of "The Promised Land," an unpublished novel, and galley proofs of "Montana Pete Goes Courting," a story not used in the 1978 edition of *Wilderness Men*. Seven letters from O'Hagan to David Robinson, editor of Talonbooks, the first written on 23 August 1977 and the last on 22 August 1978. These contain some commentary on O'Hagan's work as well as personal material.

A7   The Berkeley Arts Club Papers
     Manuscripts Division
     Bancroft Library
     University of California
     Berkeley, California
     94720

Minutes (called "chronicles") written by O'Hagan, and chronicles containing references to him.

A8   The A.J.M. Smith Papers
     Thomas Fisher Rare Book Library
     University of Toronto
     Toronto, Ontario
     M5S 1A5

Manuscripts by Howard O'Hagan: "Ursus," "The Woman Who Got On at Sacramento," "The Knife," and "A Portrait of Amy."

A9   The Diamond Jenness Papers
     Canadian Museum of Civilization
     National Museums of Canada
     Ottawa, Ontario
     K1A 0M8

A letter dated 12 December 1938 from O'Hagan to Jenness thanking him for permission to quote from *Indians of Canada* (Ottawa: National Museums of Canada, 1932).

A10  The George Woodcock Papers
     Queen's University Archives
     Kathleen Ryan Hall
     Queen's University
     Kingston, Ontario
     K7L 3N6

Letters exchanged by Woodcock and O'Hagan from June 1975 to April 1976. Correspondence between Woodcock and John Robbins of the Canadian Writers' Foundation about O'Hagan.

A11    The R.E. Watters Papers
       Special Collections
       University of British Columbia Library
       1956 Main Mall
       Vancouver, British Columbia
       V6T 1Y3

Correspondence (four letters) concerning the possible publication of "Trees Are Lonely Company" in *The British Columbia Centennial Anthology*, edited by R.E. Watters (Toronto: McClelland, 1958).

A12    The Thomas O'Hagan Records
       Whyte Museum of the Canadian Rockies
       111 Bear Street
       Box 160
       Banff, Alberta
       T0L 0C0

Tapes of an interview with O'Hagan about his father conducted in 1977 by Ted Hart.

A13    The Writers' Union of Canada Papers
       Mills Memorial Library
       McMaster University
       1280 Main Street West
       Hamilton, Ontario
       L8S 4L6

Correspondence between O'Hagan and the Writers' Union concerning his copyright to *Tay John*.

# B Contributions to Periodicals and Books: Short Stories and Sketches, Reprinted Anthology Contributions, Articles, Review, Radio Material, and Miscellaneous

NOTE: *When an item is reprinted in one of O'Hagan's books, the bibliography entry for the item will use an abbreviation of the book title. The abbreviations are:*

*Tay John* . . . . . . . . . . . . . . . . . . . . . . . . . . TJ
*Wilderness Men* . . . . . . . . . . . . . . . . . . . . . . . WM
*The Woman Who Got On at Jasper Station and Other Stories* . . JS
*The School-Marm Tree* . . . . . . . . . . . . . . . . . . . . SMT

## Short Stories and Sketches

B1  "How It Came About." *Sydney Mail* 27 July 1927: 16.

B2  "Cuidado Con Los Golpes." *John O'London's Weekly* 20 May 1938: 245–46.

B3  "A Mountain Journey." *Queen's Quarterly* 46 (1939): 324–33. Rpt. in JS (1977).

B4  "The Pool." *Story* Nov.–Dec. 1939: 42–46.

B5  "Savoir-Faire." *Maclean's* 1 Dec. 1939: 7–9, 46–47.

B6  "The Stranger." *Queen's Quarterly* 47 (1940): 296–310. Rpt. in JS (1977).

B7  "Conquest of a Rock." *Toronto Star Weekly* 22 Aug. 1942: 3.

B8  "Ito Fujika, the Trapper." *Prairie Schooner* 19 (1945): 310–17. Rpt. in JS (1963 and 1977).

B9  "The Tepee." *New Mexico Quarterly Review* 15 (1945): 304–12. Rpt. in JS (1963 and 1977).

B10  "The White Horse." *Maclean's* 1 Nov. 1945: 13, 34, 37–39. Rpt. in JS (1963 and 1977).

B11  "The Colony." *Circle* 7 (1946): 65–67.

B12  "The Love Story of Mr. Wimple." *Berkeley* 2 (1948): 3–5. Rpt. as "The Love Story of Mr. Alfred Wimple" in JS (1963 and 1977).

B13  "The Warning." *Weekend Magazine* 21 Nov. 1953: 18–19.

B14  "The Fabulous Journey." *Weekend Magazine* 13 Mar. 1954: 34.

B15  "The Warpath of Almighty Voice." *True* Mar. 1954: 29–31, 79–83.

B16  "The Mad Trapper of Rat River." *Argosy* Sept. 1954: 32–33, 81–84.

B17  "Her Father's Daughter." *Weekend Magazine* 29 Jan. 1955: 8, 18, 22, 30.

B18  "The Man Who Stayed Invisible for Thirteen Years." *Maclean's* 5 July 1958: 20–21, 34–39.

B19  "Trees Are Lonely Company." *Tamarack Review* 9 (1958): 29–45. Rpt. with revisions in JS (1963 and 1977).

B20  "Her Name . . . Was Mary." *Event* 5 (1976): 84–96.

B21  "The School-Marm Tree." *Event* 5 (1976): 49–83.

B22  "Ursus." *Malahat Review* 50 (1979): 49–64.

### Reprinted Anthology Contributions

B23  "The Tepee." *Stories from Western Canada.* Ed. Rudy Wiebe. Toronto: Macmillan, 1972. 25–34. Rpt. as "Die Indianerzelt." *Moderne Erzähler der Welt: Kanada.* Trans., ed., and introd. Walter Riedel. Tübingen: Horst Erdmann Verlag für Internationalen Kulturaustauch, 1976. 145–56.

B24  "The Fight with the Bear" [Excerpt from TJ]. *The Canadian Century: English-Canadian Writing since Confederation.* Ed. A.J.M. Smith. Toronto: Gage, 1973. 503–13. Rpt. in *The Canadian Experience: A Brief Survey of English-Canadian Prose.* Ed. A.J.M. Smith. Agincourt, ON: Gage, 1974. 146–56.

B25  "Trees Are Lonely Company." *Great Canadian Adventure Stories.* Ed. Muriel Whitaker. Edmonton: Hurtig, 1979. 151–67.

B26  "The Woman Who Got On at Jasper Station." *Alberta Diamond Jubilee Anthology.* Ed. John W. Chalmers. Edmonton: Hurtig, 1979. 75–81.

B27 "The White Horse." *More Stories from Western Canada*. Ed. Rudy Wiebe and Aritha Van Herk. Toronto: Macmillan, 1980. 1–12. Rpt. in *Skookum Wawa: Writings of the Canadian Northwest*. Ed. Gary Geddes. Toronto: Oxford UP, 1975. 3–11.

B28 "The Bride's Crossing." *Best Canadian Short Stories*. Ed. John Stevens. Toronto: McClelland, 1981. 36–45.

B29 "Ito Fujika, the Trapper." *A British Columbia Celebration*. Ed. George Woodcock. Edmonton: Hurtig, 1983. 183–86.

B30 "Ursus." *Illusion One: Fantasies and Metafictions*. Ed. Geoff Hancock. Toronto: Aya, 1983. 99–109.

B31 "Tay John" [Excerpt from TJ]. *Tales from the Canadian Rockies*. Ed. Brian Patton. Edmonton: Hurtig, 1984. 196–203.

*Articles*

B32 "The Cowboy: A Disappearing Factor." *Sydney Morning Herald* 9 Apr. 1927: 11.

B33 "Roads from Athabaska Tar Sands." *American City* Sept. 1928: 121–22.

B34 "Conquerors of Nature's Giants." *Canadian National Railways Magazine* Oct. 1930: 9.

B35 "Grizzled Gentleman." *Maclean's* 1 Jan. 1949: 11, 40–41.

B36 "The Strangest Hunt of His Life." *Argosy* May 1953: 25, 65–67.

B37 "The Wily Wraith that Trappers Hate." *Maclean's* 1 Dec. 1954: 36, 63–66.

B38 "The Ghostly Sentinel of the Peaks." *Maclean's* 26 Nov. 1955: 30–31, 46, 48, 52–53.

B39 "Nobody Has More Fun than an Otter." *Maclean's* 14 Apr. 1956: 38, 72, 74, 76.

B40 "The Bear Cub is Everybody's Baby." *Maclean's* 21 July 1956: 22–23, 34–36.

B41 "Why Have We Lost the Joy of Walking?" *Maclean's* 11 May 1957: 32, 58, 60, 62.

B42 "We Are Not Alone." *Islander* 25 Oct. 1959: 12.
*The Islander* is the weekly magazine of the Victoria *Colonist*.

B43 "Cold Disaster." *Islander* [Victoria *Colonist*] 3 Jan. 1960: 5.

B44 "The Weird and Savage Cult of Brother 12." *Maclean's* 23 Apr. 1960: 22–23, 34, 36, 39.

B45 "The Long Night." *Islander* [Victoria *Colonist*] 18 Dec. 1960: 2.

B46 "The Packhorse on the Moose?" *Islander* [Victoria *Colonist*] 7 May 1961: 12–13.

B47 "The Cubs of the Swiftwater." *Islander* [Victoria *Colonist*] 21 May 1961: 2–3.

B48 "Dwellers in the Dusk around Us." *Islander* [Victoria *Colonist*] 4 June 1961: 3, 10.

B49 "Not All the Pioneers Were Valorous Souls." *Islander* [Victoria *Colonist*] 11 June 1961: 7, 15.

B50 "Where the Tide Whispered." *Islander* [Victoria *Colonist*] 25 June 1961: 2.

B51 "Stephie." *Queen's Quarterly* 68 (1961): 135–46. Rpt. in *McGill News* 42.3 (1961): 20–22; *McGill News* 42.4 (1961): 22–24.

B52 "His Worship the Mayor." *McGill News* 44.1 (1962): 31–32.

B53 "The Trail Blazers." *Islander* [Victoria *Colonist*] 21 Oct. 1962: 4.

B54 ". . . To Follow Knowledge Like a Sinking Star. . . ." *Islander* [Victoria *Colonist*] 28 Oct. 1962: 4.

B55 "The Hard Way." *Islander* [Victoria *Colonist*] 4 Nov. 1962: 16.
This is the first of O'Hagan's "Then and Now" columns for the *Colonist*'s weekly magazine *The Islander*.

B56 "Parks Need Protection." *Islander* [Victoria *Colonist*] 11 Nov. 1962: 4.

B57 "Hero of the Long Chase." *Islander* [Victoria *Colonist*] 18 Nov. 1962: 16.

B58 "Steam Revival for the P.G.E." *Islander* [Victoria *Colonist*] 25 Nov. 1962: 3.

B59 "Woman with Her Turkeys." *Islander* [Victoria *Colonist*] 2 Dec. 1962: 3.

B60 "When She-Bear Asked for Help." *Islander* [Victoria *Colonist*] 9 Dec. 1962: 10.

B61 "The Chinese Laughed." *Islander* [Victoria *Colonist*] 16 Dec. 1962: 11.

B62 "Death Lurks in Silence." *Islander* [Victoria *Colonist*] 23 Dec. 1962: 12.

B63 "Coyote's Song to Perish?" *Islander* [Victoria *Colonist*] 30 Dec. 1962: 13.

B64 "Strange Portents on a Mountain Trail." *Islander* [Victoria *Colonist*] 6 Jan. 1963: 16.

B65 "The Man Who Took Chilcotin to Australia." *Islander* [Victoria *Colonist*] 13 Jan. 1963: 5.

B66 "Man in a Bear Trap." *Islander* [Victoria *Colonist*] 20 Jan. 1963: 13.

B67 "Pushing Back the Frontier." *Islander* [Victoria *Colonist*] 27 Jan. 1963: 3.

B68 "Reach Up . . . towards the Stars!" *Islander* [Victoria *Colonist*] 3 Feb. 1963: 16.

B69 "Breakfasts Must Be Eaten Alone." *Islander* [Victoria *Colonist*] 10 Feb. 1963: 3.

B70 "Color Bar in Canada." *Islander* [Victoria *Colonist*] 17 Feb. 1963: 11.

B71 "Bannock Baker." *Islander* [Victoria *Colonist*] 24 Feb. 1963: 16.

B72 "A Secret in the Barn." *Islander* [Victoria *Colonist*] 3 Mar. 1963: 5.

B73 "Little Duck Abandoned." *Islander* [Victoria *Colonist*] 10 Mar. 1963: 11.

B74 "For Every Mile a Life Was Taken." *Islander* [Victoria *Colonist*] 17 Mar. 1963: 12.

B75 "What's Wrong with Walking?" *Islander* [Victoria *Colonist*] 14 Apr. 1963: 2.

B76 "Death at His Heels." *Islander* [Victoria *Colonist*] 21 Apr. 1963: 11.

B77 "Slow Men Working." *Islander* [Victoria *Colonist*] 28 Apr. 1963: 16.

B78 "Diesel Locos Came to Stay." *Islander* [Victoria *Colonist*] 5 May 1963: 13.

B79 "The Artist Has a Language All Her Own." *Islander* [Victoria *Colonist*] 12 May 1963: 5.

B80 "Writers Need Experience!" *Islander* [Victoria *Colonist*] 2 June 1963: 11.

B81 "Train-Running: My Most Strenuous Crossing of Canada." *Times* [Victoria, BC] 12 Sept. 1963: 4.

## Review

B82 "New Voice in the Wilderness." Rev. of *Royal Murdoch* by Robert Harlow. *Colonist* [Victoria, BC] 30 Dec. 1962: 15.

## Radio Material

B83 "Trees Are Lonely Company." Read by David Hughes. *Anthology*. CBC. 24 Apr. 1956; rebroadcast 20 Oct. 1961.

B84 "The Stranger." Read by John Drainie. *Anthology*. CBC. 30 Oct. 1956.

B85 "The Teepee." *Anthology*. CBC. [1956?]

B86 "A Mountain Journey." Read by Budd Knapp. *Anthology*. CBC. 11 Mar. 1958.

B87 "The Knife." Read by David Hughes. *Anthology*. CBC. 25 May 1962.

*Miscellaneous*

B88   Letter. "Save the Grizzlies." *Vancouver Sun* 16 July 1957: 4.

B89   Letter. "Statement Disclaimed." *Colonist* [Victoria, BC] 20 July 1958: 5.

## *Part II*   WORKS ON HOWARD O'HAGAN

C   Books, Articles and Sections of Books, Thesis, Interviews, Miscellaneous, and Awards and Honours

### *Books*

C1   Tanner, Ella. *Tay John and the Cyclical Quest: The Shape of Art and Vision in Howard O'Hagan.* Toronto: ECW, 1990. 165 pp.
   Tanner feels O'Hagan catches sight of a spiritual essence: "O'Hagan's vision appears to evolve intuitively in accordance with Jung's conception of God as an archtypal image in which opposites are reconciled." A revised version of C39.

C2   Asai, Akira. *Asian Shadows in Canadian Literature: A Comparative Study on Howard O'Hagan's* Tay John." Tokyo: NCI, 1986. 24 pp.
   Asai first compares the myth of Tay John's birth with a famous Japanese story, "Kosodate Yurei," about a ghost who raises her baby in a grave, suggesting the similarities are the result of "some physical contacts of the different cultures across the Pacific." He then compares Julia Alderson's accusations against Tay John and Miss Quested's against Aziz in E. M. Forster's *A Passage to India* (1924).

### *Articles and Sections of Books*

C3   Cash, Gwen. "Mountain Man." *Province* [Vancouver, BC] 23 Nov. 1957: 3.

C4   _____ . "Man of the Mountains." *Colonist* [Victoria, BC] 13 July 1958: 11. Slightly revised version of C3.

C5 Fergusson, Harvey. Introduction. *Tay John*. New York: Potter, 1960. N. pag. Rpt. in *Tay John*. New Canadian Library 105. Toronto: McClelland, 1974. N. pag.

The "blending of the mythical and the legendary with the humanly real and moving is perhaps the chief technical achievement of the story but its unique quality springs from an unusual knowledge and experience of the land and the people O'Hagan writes about. . . . He was never a hunter nor a trapper but only a wanderer who loved wilderness for its own sake, saw it with the eye of an artist, and imbued its mystery with an artist's imagination."

C6 Jones, D.G. *Butterfly on Rock: A Study of Themes and Images in Canadian Literature.* Toronto: U of Toronto P, 1970. 7, ff.

Jones discusses the symbolic role of the "half-breed" and the significance of religion in the novel.

C7 Smith, A.J.M. "Howard O'Hagan, 1902– ." *The Canadian Century: English-Canadian Writing since Confederation.* Ed. Smith. Toronto: Gage, 1973. 503. Rpt. in *The Canadian Experience: A Brief Survey of English-Canadian Prose.* Ed. Smith. Agincourt, ON: Gage, 1974. 146.

"Howard O'Hagan is perhaps the least-known Canadian writer of superior excellence. The episode from *Tay John* included here ["The Fight with the Bear"] is an unforgettable masterpiece."

C8 Morley, Patricia. "Introduction to the New Canadian Library Edition." *Tay John*. 1960. New Canadian Library 105. Toronto: McClelland, 1974. vii–xiv.

A useful examination of image patterns, plot structure, and humour in the novel: "the wilderness that concerns O'Hagan more closely than the Rocky Mountain terrain is the human personality. . . ."

C9 Ondaatje, Michael. "O'Hagan's Rough-Edged Chronicle." *Canadian Literature* 61 (1974): 24–31. Rpt. in *The Canadian Novel in the Twentieth Century.* Ed. George Woodcock. Toronto: McClelland, 1975. 276–84.

This important article emphasizes the central image of *Tay John*, which is "birth from and eventual disappearance into the earth." It compares O'Hagan's narrators with Conrad's: "I can think of no novel that has got as close to that raw power of myth as O'Hagan's book does."

C10  Atwood, Margaret. "Canadian Monsters." *The Canadian Imagination: Dimensions of a Literary Culture*. Ed. David Staines. Cambridge: Harvard UP, 1977. 97–122 [see esp. 104–06]. Rpt. in *Other Canadas: An Anthology of Science Fiction and Fantasy*. Ed. J.R. Colombo. Toronto: McGraw-Hill, 1979. 333–51; *Second Words: Selected Critical Prose*. By Atwood. Toronto: Anansi, 1982. 229–53.

This is the text of a lecture given by Atwood at Harvard University in 1976. Atwood compares Tay John to figures in novels by Sheila Watson and P.K. Page, among others: "in at least two Canadian novels the protagonist is a semi-human being. . . . A case in point is the central character in *Tay John*, Howard O'Hagan's potent and disturbing novel."

C11  Geddes, Gary. "The Writer That CanLit Forgot." *Saturday Night* Nov. 1977: 84–92.

An excellent account that combines interview, biography, and critical insight: "O'Hagan . . . has the stamp of a natural story-teller, which, in a writer, requires an enormous talent and hard work. Much truth, whether sought for or unbidden, has come to this passionate, sometimes irascible old man."

C12  Harrison, Dick. *Unnamed Country: The Struggle for a Canadian Prairie Fiction*. Edmonton: U of Alberta P, 1977. ix, ff.

Harrison's title is taken from *Tay John*. Harrison uses O'Hagan as a starting point for his discussion of western Canadian literature.

C13  Page, P.K. Introduction. *The School-Marm Tree*. Vancouver: Talonbooks, 1977. 7–10.

"Despite its title, its plot, its portrait of the past, *The School-Marm Tree* is really a novel about that mountain presence and the quality of heart capable of discerning it. From first to last — inspiring or threatening — the omnipresent mountains dominate. And Selva, dreaming girl, is the delicate instrument through which we sense and respond to the presence they conjure up."

C14  Monkman, Leslie. *A Native Heritage: Images of the Indian in English-Canadian Literature*. Toronto: U of Toronto P, 1981. 44–48.

Tay John's conflicts are "essentially religious." Tay John and Ardith Aeriola must retreat "from the materialism and corruption of the white man's world, a world lacking both spiritual principles and, as the deaths of the Rorty brothers indicate, adequate spiritual guides."

C15  Moss, John. *A Reader's Guide to Canadian Literature.* Toronto: McClelland, 1981. 221–22. Rpt. in the 2nd ed., 1987. 284–86. [No changes were made to the O'Hagan entry.]

Like many of the early reviewers, Moss falls for the artfully "crude" aspects of the novel and for Fergusson's selective account of O'Hagan's life in the introduction to the 1960 edition: "*Tay John* draws heavily on western Indian mythology, with a strong infusion of the Christian, but is entirely a new creation, one fortunately undisciplined by convention or rationality."

C16  Davidson, Arnold E. "Being and Definition in Howard O'Hagan's *Tay John*." *Études Canadiennes* 15 (1983): 137–47.

This is the first article to note the novel's avant-garde qualities: "Just as O'Hagan anticipates especially the French existentialists who wrote shortly after World War II, so too does he anticipate more contemporary theories of narratology and the self-reflexive nature of articulation."

C17  Geddes, Gary. "British Columbia, Writing in." *The Oxford Companion to Canadian Literature.* Ed. William Toye. Toronto: Oxford UP, 1983.

*Tay John* "is the most important work of fiction to come out of British Columbia before the Second World War. . . . [I]t can be called Canada's first serious work of metafiction. . . . O'Hagan's treatment . . . lays the foundations for such future myth-makers as Sheila Watson, Robert Harlow, Rudy Wiebe, Robert Kroetsch, and Jack Hodgins."

C18  Hancock, Geoff. "O'Hagan, Howard." *The Oxford Companion to Canadian Literature.* Ed. William Toye. Toronto: Oxford UP, 1983.

"O'Hagan's writings are dominated by the Rocky Mountains. As he continued to write, even though he suffered from the lack of a supportive community, he became known as the mountain man of Canadian letters — and one of the best prose writers of western Canada. He has had a strong influence on Rudy Wiebe, Robert Harlow, Jack Hodgins, Don Gutteridge, and Michael Ondaatje. . . ."

C19  Nowosad, Frank. "The Turmoil of Creative Activity." *Monday Magazine* [Victoria, BC] 6 May 1983: 19–22.

Nowosad discusses the art and ideas of O'Hagan and his wife, Margaret Peterson: "Apart from their fascination and respect for the natural and spiritual qualities in early art, the work of Howard O'Hagan and Margaret Peterson takes divergent paths. His writing tends to fable and parable; her painting and drawing to a particular, sophisticated abstraction."

C20  Colombo, J.R. *Canadian Literary Landmarks*. Willowdale, ON: Hounslow, 1984. 245, 254–55.
Brief accounts of the Yellowhead Pass area and of Howard O'Hagan are given.

C21  Harrison, Dick. "The Deep Pool of the Unconscious: *The Man Who Killed the Deer* and *Tay John*." *Studies in Frank Waters VII: An Appreciation*. Ed. and introd. Charles L. Adams. Proc. of a Conjoint Meeting of the Frank Waters Society and Rocky Mountain Modern Language Association. 17–19 Oct. 1985. Las Vegas: Frank Waters Society, 1985. 45–55.
This comparison of Frank Waters's novel with O'Hagan's focuses on the symbolism of lakes. The central characters in both novels are torn between Native and white culture. Waters's hero finds what may be only an "interim solution," while "Tay John's fate suggests an ultimately irreconcilable conflict between civilized and natural worlds."

C22  Keith, W.J. *Canadian Literature in English*. London: Longman, 1985. 138–39.
Keith discusses O'Hagan's similarities to Conrad, and concludes that O'Hagan is "a powerful writer, with unusual gifts ([*The School-Marm Tree*] is an extended fable, elemental and almost Lawrentian in tone . . .). It is, however, for *Tay John* that he will be remembered."

C23  Stouck, David. "The Art of the Mountain Man Novel." *Western American Literature* 20 (1985): 211–22.
Stouck connects *Tay John* with a subgenre of the American Western familiar to O'Hagan through *Wolf Song* (1927), written by his friend Harvey Fergusson: *Tay John*, "through symbolism and a circular, indirect narration, succeeds perhaps more than others in suggesting the primitive area of the mountain man's violent nature."

C24  Davidson, Arnold E. "Silencing the Word in Howard O'Hagan's *Tay John*." *Canadian Literature* 110 (1986): 31–44.
This article concludes that there is a great chasm between words and objects in the novel: "Words, in short, do not lead to any truths in or of the novel, and the text marks out a space of misnaming and misunderstanding." Davidson discusses parallels and contrasts in *Tay John* and the Gospels.

C25  Fee, Margery. "Howard O'Hagan's *Tay John*: Making New World Myth." *Canadian Literature* 110 (1986): 8–27.

Fee focuses on O'Hagan's conviction that "no story is complete," concluding that in making this point, "O'Hagan undermines to varying degrees several dominant and interconnected Western ideologies: idealism, Christianity, patriarchy, class, and capitalism. . . . O'Hagan's replacement of divine authority in the making of myth, indeed his replacement of even a human author by a collective 'intertextuality' connects him to post-structuralism."

C26  Fenton, William. "Parody in O'Hagan's *Tay John*." *Canada: Ieri e oggi 2*. Ed. Giovanni Bonnanno. Atti del 6 Convegno Internazionale di Studi Canadesi. [*Canada: Yesterday and Today 2*. Proc. of the Sixth International Conference in Canadian Studies. English-Language Sessions.] 27–31 Marzo 1985. Bari: Schena, 1986. 55–73.

Tay John takes certain modernist positions; he shows "a concern with the opposition between language as creator of myth and the myth of language as an instrument capable of defining truth and naming that which cannot be named." Fenton takes Linda Hutcheon's definition of parody from her *A Theory of Parody* (1985) to examine the novel's combination of the heroic and the ludicrous.

C27  Carrington, Ildikó de Papp. "Margaret Atwood." *Canadian Writers and Their Works*. Fiction Series. Ed. Robert Lecker, Jack David, and Ellen Quigley. Vol. 9. Downsview, ON: ECW, 1987. 25–116 [see esp. 63–64]. 10 vols. 1983–92.

Carrington discusses connections between *Tay John*, Atwood's *Surfacing*, and P.K. Page's *The Sun and the Moon and Other Stories*.

C28  Fenton, William. "The Past and Mythopoesis." *Re-Writing the Past: History and Origin in Howard O'Hagan, Jack Hodgins, George Bowering and Chris Scott*. I Quattro Continenti 1. Rome: Bulzoni, 1988. 15–64.

Fenton uses the theories of an array of poststructuralist critics to analyze *Tay John*, concluding that "Each person's version of the story is an attempt to define the truth, to reach an origin, but as the text has demonstrated truth is a fiction, fiction is the essence of myth, and myths like Tay John's contain the truth of the region's past."

C29  Mitchell, Ken. "O'Hagan, Howard." *The Canadian Encyclopedia*. 2nd ed. Edmonton: Hurtig, 1988.

"More than any other modern writer, O'Hagan has been the quint-essential 'mountain man' who knew the wilderness intimately and celebrated it through fiction."

C30 Robinson, Jack. "Myths of Dominance vs. Myths of Re-Creation in O'Hagan's *Tay John.*" *Studies in Canadian Literature* 13.2 (1988): 166–74.
"In Barthes' terms, O'Hagan has created not a 'work' designed to appeal to the presumptions of his culture, but a 'text' which gives pleasure by 'deconstructing' those premises, especially the world-explaining myth of ideology itself."

C31 Skelton, Robin. *The Memoirs of a Literary Blockhead.* Toronto: Macmillan, 1988. 166–67.
This book contains a brief anecdote about O'Hagan's response to a play by Rona Murray.

C32 Stouck, David. *Major Canadian Authors: A Critical Introduction.* 2nd rev. ed. Lincoln: U of Nebraska P, 1988. 98, 290.
"The experience and vision of the mountain man constitutes a rela-tively small portion of Canadian literature, but in Howard O'Hagan's *Tay John,* a mythic tale of a half-breed Indian, and in the poetry of Earle Birney and Patrick Lane it has found particularly eloquent expression."

C33 Keith, W.J. "Howard O'Hagan." *A Sense of Style: Studies in the Art of Fiction in English-Speaking Canada.* Toronto: ECW, 1989. 23–39.
O'Hagan uses a form between fiction and nonfiction that allows him to transform "yarn into serious art." Keith includes O'Hagan in his discussion "to counter the prevailing assumption that serious Canadian fiction in English began with *As for Me and My House* and MacLennan's *Barometer Rising,*" and "because O'Hagan's treatment of story seems to be crucial for an understanding of certain special features relating to Canadian fiction."

C34 Kroetsch, Robert. "The Veil of Knowing." *The Lovely Treachery of Words: Essays Selected and New.* Toronto: Oxford UP, 1989. 179–94.
Kroetsch examines the way *Tay John* conceals rather than reveals meaning as paradigmatic of Canadian literature more generally: "Cana-dian literature, at its most radical, is the autobiography of a culture that tells its story by telling us repeatedly it has no story to tell. Jack Denham — or perhaps Tay John — is the emblem of this condition. Jack becomes

John becomes Jack." *Tay John* is compared to several other novels, including George Bowering's *Burning Water* (1980), Sheila Watson's *The Double Hook* (1959), and Ernest Buckler's *The Mountain and the Valley* (1952).

C35 Ondaatje, Michael. Afterword. *Tay John.* 1960. New Canadian Library 105. Toronto: McClelland, 1989. 265–72.

O'Hagan's style, Ondaatje maintains, is "mythic realism" rather than "magic realism." In *Tay John* "the hero's tale is left intact, and the source of the legend is never qualified." Ondaatje also sets the novel at the head of a peripheral tradition of Canadian novels that reject "the realistic tradition that seems to continue endlessly and without wit." Included in his peripheral tradition are *Tay John* (1939), Elizabeth Smart's *By Grand Central Station I Sat Down and Wept* (1945), Ethel Wilson's *Swamp Angel* (1954), and Sheila Watson's *The Double Hook* (1959).

C36 Scobie, Stephen. *Signature, Event, Cantext.* Edmonton: NeWest, 1989. 141.

*Tay John* is briefly examined in the context of Jacques Derrida's theories: "Every version of 'beginning' that *Tay John* holds out is subsequently seen to be a trace (deferral, supplement) of something that went before."

C37 Beddoes, Julie. "The Train We Mythed: Crossed Lines in Howard O'Hagan's *Tay John.*" *Open Letter* 7th ser. 7 (1990): 74–83.

The theories of Barthes and Derrida are used to explore the tension between myth in its traditional definition as a unifying force and in Barthes's sense as a "type of speech chosen by history." Beddoes concludes that "those who are waiting for the great train ride from mother earth to contemporary reality might do better on another narrative line," noting that both the novel's myths and its symbolic railway are more likely to disintegrate into textual fragments than produce a unitary whole.

C38 Robinson, Jack. "Dismantling Sexual Dualities: O'Hagan's *Tay John.*" *Alberta* 2.2 (1990): 93–108.

Robinson gives a brief biography of O'Hagan, and reviews the major articles on *Tay John* to date, before setting out his major argument: "One of the innovative strengths of *Tay John* is its analysis of how the sexual dualities of spirit/body, possessor/possessed, civilized/natural, and maternal/adult love create and perpetuate agonizing self-divisions and sexual antagonisms."

*Thesis*

C39 Tanner, Ella. "*Tay John*: The Cyclical Quest. The Shape of Art and Vision in Howard O'Hagan." MA thesis. Concordia, 1987. Revised as C1.

Tanner sees Tay John as mythic rather than metafictional: "[U]nlike many magic-realist and metafictional texts, *Tay John* is not a reinvention of the world, but a reorientation to it, an original vitalization of the primitive, a recovery of its spirit and power."

*Interviews*

C40 Mitchell, Ken. "Wilderness Man." *Sound Heritage* 5 (1976): 22–25.

An unedited tape of this interview is held in the British Columbia Provincial Archives, Victoria. O'Hagan tells anecdotes about guiding and packing in the Rockies as a young man.

C41 Roberts, Kevin. "Talking to Howard O'Hagan." *Event* 5 (1976): 41–48.

An account of Roberts's meeting with O'Hagan at a reading, and of a subsequent visit with Howard and Margaret O'Hagan.

C42 Wigod, Rebecca. "How a Man of Wilderness Became a Man of Words." *Times-Colonist* [Victoria, BC] 9 July 1982: 21.

O'Hagan tells of an early visit to a cabin in the foothills of the Rocky Mountains, where he met the real-life "Montana Pete." He says that the mountain man's tales inspired two early short stories. Speaking about *Tay John*, O'Hagan remarks: "I accept my short stories, but that novel is full of flaws."

*Miscellaneous*

C43 "Respected Author Dies." Obituary. *Times-Colonist* [Victoria, BC] 21 Sept. 1982: B8.

C44 Obituary. *Quill & Quire* Dec. 1982: 13.

## Awards and Honours

C45   President's Medal from the University of Western Ontario for the Best Short Story Published in 1958, "Trees Are Lonely Company" (B13) (1959).

C46   Canada Council Senior Arts Bursary (1976).

C47   Honorary Member, Writers' Union of Canada (1976–82).

C48   D.Litt., McGill University (1982).

## D   Selected Book Reviews

TAY JOHN

D1   "Backwoods Mythology." Rev. of *Tay John*. *Times Literary Supplement* 18 Mar. 1939: 166.
   "Mr. Howard O'Hagan has so skilfully presented this tale . . . and he has so closely interwoven with it the spirit of the forests and lakes and the long white silences, that legend merges into the narrative of actual happenings, and the ghostly figure of the child who had no shadow seems natural father to the man who 'just walked down, the toboggan behind him, under the snow and into the ground.' This is an odd, compelling story and one that is likely to live on in the mind."

D2   Swinnerton, Frank. "New Novels." Rev. of *Tay John*. *Observer* [London] 19 Mar. 1939: 6.
   "The one novel in my batch which stirs romantic longings is 'Tay John,' the pieced or episodic history of a half-breed Indian from his childhood with the tribe to his death in a snowy waste. It is a vivid panorama which begins in the vein of folk tale and proceeds by several contributory narratives as the life-history of a man. We see Tay John learning his job as trapper and guide; we watch his fight with a grizzly bear and the scene in which he is charged, incredibly, with rape, and how he disappeared into the mountains with a woman of the cities. Mr.

O'Hagan, who does not like English M.P.s, writes with force; and some of the backgrounds are seen with decided intensity. They, rather than the character of Tay John, make the book a living picture, but the man himself is there as well." [This is the complete review.]

D3 D'Easum, G.C. Rev. of *Tay John*. *Province* [Vancouver] 15 Apr. 1939: 4.

"Your reviewer, in the early [18]90s, knew well 'the small wooden church by the dirt road' and the heroic little man who ministered there. But surely the 'first hotel,' haunt of those lovable rascals, the remittance men, was called the 'Hotel Jasper,' the name of the principal street in Edmonton today?"

D4 Rev. of *Tay John*. *Canadian Forum* Sept. 1939: 199.

"Tête Jaune, or Tay John, was the tall fair son of an Indian woman. His conspicuous appearance and his exploits among the Indians and the white men who came to the west during railway-building days made his name a by-word and his birth a legend. He loves the strange foreign girl and dies a lonely death for her. One seems to have read it all before." [This is the complete review.]

D5 MacGillivray, J.R. "Letters in Canada: Fiction." Rev. of *Tay John*. *University of Toronto Quarterly* 9 (1939–40): 299.

"Tay John, based on an Indian legend and the author's acquaintance with the Rocky Mountain hinterland, is excellent in narrative and good in description, but confused and confusing in development and undistinguished in characterization."

D6 Keate, Stuart. "Intruder in the Wilderness." Rev. of *Tay John*. *New York Times Book Review* 13 Mar. 1960: 34.

"Few writers have been able to put down on paper as well as [O'Hagan] the power, the beauty and the loneliness of this country, with its towering peaks, amethyst lakes, and restless wildlife. In a curiously groping but sensitive style he has captured the first intrusions of man on a wilderness, and in so doing has contrived a tale of mystic charm and distinction."

D7 Rev. of *Tay John*. *Booklist* 15 Mar. 1960: 444.

"An absorbing novel reminiscent of a folk tale focuses on the part-Indian Tay John who abandons his role as tribal leader and becomes a solitary trapper in the mountains of Western Canada. . . . The author's knowledge of outdoor life lends additional authenticity to a story set in the late nineteenth and early twentieth centuries."

D8  Schmuck, John. Rev. of *Tay John*. *Library Journal* 1 Apr. 1960: 1474.
Tay John "remains mysterious to the reader, effectively so, even as he cuts off a hand to acquire a horse or becomes involved with a European woman of easy virtue. The mood of the wilderness is always maintained and the writing is of a generally high level; the only real fault is Mr. O'Hagan's tendency at times to be a bit heavy-handed with his symbolism."

D9  Mayhew, Anne. Rev. of *Tay John*. *Stylus* [University of Victoria] Nov. 1960: n. pag.
"If fatalism and mysticism can meet, they are brought together here in the legend of Tay John."

D10  Robertson, George. "Mountain Man Mythology." Rev. of *Tay John*. *Canadian Literature* 9 (1961): 65–66.
A generally unfavourable review, which, nonetheless, notes many of the novel's distinctive features: "The strain, the consciousness of verbal elaboration, is an irritating presence between ourselves and the story, and . . . we are always brought around to the author saying 'Here is myth in the making.' "

D11  Watt, F.W. "Letters in Canada: Fiction." Rev. of *Tay John*. *University of Toronto Quarterly* 30 (1961): 414–15.
The novel is "a somewhat incoherent fictional illustration of how myths might come into being, beginning as it does with an Indian legend, and progressing (with increasing realism: legend, hearsay, evidence) to the adventures of the half-breed Tay John. . . . The book has moments of strangeness and excitement, but as Tay John becomes less mysterious so the work becomes more a sequence of melodramatic yarns without satisfactory resolution."

D12  Woodcock, George. "You Can't Judge a Book by Its Past." Rev. of new titles in the New Canadian Library Series. *Maclean's* May 1974: 100.
"Howard O'Hagan's *Tay John*, a splendid tale of a mythical Rocky Mountain half-breed hero, is particularly welcome. It was published in 1960 and has never received the attention it deserves as an imaginative and beautifully constructed book."

D13 Stow, Glenys. "A Discordant Heritage." Rev. of *Tay John. Journal of Canadian Fiction* 16 (1976): 178–81.

"The novel is concerned . . . with varieties of illusion . . . but there are degrees of illusion, and to O'Hagan the man who keeps close to natural instincts, the primitive world and wilderness keeps close also to heroic stature, while those seduced by the dream of mechanized progress grow demonic."

WILDERNESS MEN

D14 Rev. of *Wilderness Men. Kirkus Reviews* 15 May 1958: 369.

"This is an account of ten men of the West — exiles — three Indians, seven white men, who met life alone, in the forests of the Pacific slopes, in the Rockies, on the northern prairies or in the wastes of the Arctic. . . . Each episode is related in a highly-dramatized manner which occasionally creates more hyperbole than drama."

D15 Oboler, Eli. Rev. of *Wilderness Men. Library Journal* July 1958: 2045.

"Among the more reputable biographees are John Colter, discoverer of Yellowstone, Grey Owl, the best-selling 'Indian' author who turned out to be an Englishman named Archie, and David Douglas, mountain-climber and botanist of the early 1800s after whom the Douglas fir was named. Competently told by a Canadian who is well acquainted with both the terrain and the people of whom he writes."

D16 Rev. of *Wilderness Men. Booklist* 1 Oct. 1958: 71.

"A trapper wanted by the Royal Canadian Mounted Police, a vengeful Indian leader, and an adventurous Scottish botanist are among the ten men described in accounts that range in time from the nineteenth to the twentieth century and have western Canada and the U.S. Northwest as backgrounds. Dramatically written, colorful true stories that contribute both courageous and notorious episodes to the wilderness saga."

D17 Keate, Stuart. "With Trap-Line and Gold Pan." Rev. of *Wilderness Men. New York Times Book Review* 19 Oct. 1958: 48.

"Mr. O'Hagan has gone to the Royal Canadian Mounted Police files or other authentic sources for his documentation. The result is a series of corking adventure stories, written with sensitivity and a healthy admiration for men who can hunt and fight (and even make love) in 60-below weather."

**D18**  Peel, Bruce. Rev. of *Wilderness Men. Saskatchewan History* 13 (1960): 79.

"O'Hagan, who is himself a wilderness man, has a fine feeling for the silent places and a thorough understanding of the psychology of men who chose to live far from the haunts of men. He is a pleasing raconteur. *Wilderness Men* can be recommended either as good historical biography or exciting adventure. . . ."

WILDERNESS MEN [2nd ed.]

**D19**  Markin, Allan. Rev. of *Wilderness Men. Canadian Book Review Annual.* Toronto: Peter Martin, 1978. 30–31.

"*Wilderness Men* has about it a schoolboyish quality — it is a sleepy book which reads like a student essay. This is so because O'Hagan's prose is shot through with clichés of culture and diction. . . . *Wilderness Men* will provide readers with many interesting facts about Canadian history. . . . Unfortunately, O'Hagan's unimaginative style prevents him from turning those facts into stories which delight as well as instruct."

**D20**  Kellythorne, Walt. "The Men of Frontier." Rev. of *Wilderness Men. Times* [Victoria, BC] 24 Feb. 1979: 13.

"O'Hagan is at his most passionate and ironic when he writes of the destruction of the native way of life. . . . These stories should be read by anyone interested in our incredible history — and present! Real people made that history, and O'Hagan captures their very breath here. A kind of immortality results."

**D21**  Morash, Gordon. "Daring-Do." Rev. of *Wilderness Men. NeWest Review* Feb. 1979: 9.

"It has been only two years since Howard O'Hagan began to be touted as an underground grand old man of letters. In spite of the drawbacks O'Hagan's mix of drama and history often makes, I still enjoy reading him. He reminds me of the Jack London stories I read as a boy, but he also speaks with the voice of wisdom and empathy. He wears the label of natural story teller well. I'd rather his history than Pierre Berton's."

**D22**  W., H.M. Rev. of *Wilderness Men. CRNLE Reviews Journal* Oct. 1979: 85–86.

"These nine stories about Canadian 'Wilderness men' are eminently readable. The subjects, verifiably historical, are fictionalized by O'Hagan who has reconstructed their lives, thoughts, motives, imaginatively. It is reality tinged with myth and told with an epic, perhaps more truly, a ballad-like detachment."

D23  Hancock, Geoff. "Short Stories Back with a Bang." Rev. of *Wilderness Men. Toronto Star* 31 Mar. 1979: D7.

"Though these stories are actually biographies of real-life men, the intensity of O'Hagan's style forces a near-mythical quality upon them, creating an air of unreality about them in much the same way American filmmakers have done for Wyatt Earp or Jesse James."

THE WOMAN WHO GOT ON AT JASPER STATION

D24  Arrol, Ed. Rev. of *The Woman Who Got On at Jasper Station. Times* [Victoria, BC] 26 Sept. 1964: 8.

"Howard O'Hagan's fiction speaks the truth about this part of Canada in a loud clear voice."

THE SCHOOL-MARM TREE *and* THE WOMAN WHO GOT ON AT JASPER STATION [1977 Talonbooks eds.; abbr. SMT and JS]

D25  Thompson, John. Rev. of SMT and JS. *Globe and Mail* 4 Mar. 1978: 41.

Discusses the influence of D.H. Lawrence and T.S. Eliot on O'Hagan: "[SMT] is quite unlike *Tay John*. Both are set in the Rockies, but where the earlier work is mythic, *The School-Marm Tree* is realistic, ordinary in almost every way. . . . [It] is testimony to his intelligence as a novelist, for he has what D.H. Lawrence saw in Hardy: a deep sensuous understanding." The strength of JS is in its stories about mountain men and sexual encounters.

D26  Fischman, Sheila. "A Mountain Celebration." Rev. of SMT and JS. *Montreal Star* 11 Mar. 1978: 39.

"Despite the tree in the title and despite the rather conventional love story that makes up the plot, [SMT] is really about mountains — about the reality of mountains that becomes so acute, so poignant, they enter, almost, into myth. Although I found most of the stories in *Jasper Station* simply dazzling, there were three that didn't quite work. . . . In the title story, a woman gets on a train and sits with a young sailor; there is a mutual attraction but there is also something missing, some elusive truth, some unanswered question, that leaves one unsatisfied."

**D27**  Powers, Gordon. "Of Men vs. Mountains, Minus Machismo." Rev. of SMT and JS. *Citizen* [Ottawa] 11 Mar. 1978: 42.

"O'Hagan's heroes desire to live by what they have, not, as do many city-dwellers, for what they lack. . . . Most of the stories [in JS] are about lonely men battling adversity in the wilds, but they carefully avoid Boy's World philosophizing and True Adventure machismo. . . . [SMT] curiously combines Harlequin romance and early Jack London. It is hackneyed and meandering, lacking the sharp focus of his short stories. . . . [It] has very little to recommend it, particularly compared to the companion volume, or O'Hagan's first novel. . . ."

**D28**  Cook, Barrie. "Cook's Books: O'Hagan Finally Getting Recognition at 75." Rev. of JS. *Province* [Vancouver] 17 Mar. 1978: 17.

"O'Hagan is a craftsman. He knows his country and writes about it beautifully. He also knows people and he can sum up the essence of a man with a few well-chosen words."

**D29**  Minni, C.D. "Clap Hands for a Canadian Classic." Rev. of SMT and JS. *Vancouver Sun* 17 Mar. 1978: 39.

"*The School-Marm Tree* is a novel which one can read and re-read and each time discover some new meaning. By comparison, *The Woman Who Got On at Jasper Station* is a mediocre collection . . . typical of magazine fiction of the pre-television era. . . . The best [stories in JS] deal with racial tensions. . . ."

**D30**  Woodcock, George. "Howard O'Hagan and Living Wilderness." Rev. of SMT and JS. *Times* [Victoria, BC] 18 Mar. 1978: 14.

"O'Hagan in [SMT] is perhaps the first writer in Canada to understand the great interior mountains with sufficient insight to draw out their nature, the brooding spirit of the landscape, in the same way as it is present in Indian legend. In this sense he was very much like his counterpart on Vancouver Island, Roderick Haig-Brown. . . . One welcomes again the stories that make up *The Woman Who Got On at Jasper Station*. . . . Most of them have an extraordinary economy and cohesion. . . . The situations are too extreme, usually, for character to be part of the episode. . . . At their best these stories are as stark as anything Camus or Sartre wrote. . . ."

**D31**  Bishop, Dorothy. "A Dramatic Silhouette." Rev. of SMT. *Journal* [Ottawa] 25 Mar. 1978: 50.

"Around [a] spare plot the author weaves a tapestry threaded by violence and by longing. His brilliant colours are as vivid in moments of stopped time as in the rush of swift movement."

D32  Novak, Barbara. Rev. of SMT and JS. *London Free Press* 25 Mar. 1978: B4.

"[The] realistic, simple plot [of SMT] has more in common with the author's short stories, which may be compared to Faulkner's in their poetic ability to capture the rich spirit of the land. . . . O'Hagan's insight into the female experience is as rare, sensitive, and profound as is his understanding of nature." The stories in JS are "excellent companion pieces to the novels."

D33  Hill, Jane W. "The Man Who Digs Mountains." Rev. of SMT and JS. *Books in Canada* Apr. 1978: 17–18.

"O'Hagan is especially fine in his understanding of women, their feelings and their place in this masculine world. Technically I think the only flaw [in SMT] is in the false foreshadowing regarding Slim; the author seems to be preparing him to be the villain but he never does become so. [SMT] is a haunting book that reverberates in the reader's mind for a long time. Humour is not much in evidence [in JS] — when O'Hagan does attempt it, as in 'The Love Story of Mr. Alfred Wimple,' I don't think he is so successful. But I can't imagine a more powerful or moving description of what it is like to die of exposure to the cold than 'A Mountain Journey.' . . ."

D34  Howard, Blanche. Rev. of SMT and JS. *Quill & Quire* Apr. 1978: 36.

"Not all of the stories in *Jasper Station* are successful. . . . The overall quality of the stories, however, is such that the reader is well rewarded. I'm afraid as much cannot be said for O'Hagan's novel, *The School-Marm Tree*. It begins beautifully: for about the first ten chapters O'Hagan's perception of the inner workings of Selva's mind is so true that it invites comparison with Sinclair Ross's *As For Me and My House*. . . . The two books have been done up handsomely as companion pieces in quality paperbacks, with Haida motif covers designed by Margaret Peterson, who is Howard O'Hagan's wife."

D35  Morash, Gordon. "Life, Death and Struggle." Rev. of SMT and JS. *NeWest Review* Apr. 1978: 9.

"There are no frills to [the] stories [of JS] — no pyrotechnics or literary feats of endurance. They're told simply and quickly and therein lies their strength. They're so tight that it's possible to miss their finer points. The stories that succeed the best are the ones dealing with what O'Hagan knows best — life, death and struggle in the mountains. . . . Of *The School-Marm Tree*, perhaps it is best to say that as fine as the individual bits are they do not make up for a satisfying whole. The skill O'Hagan shows for the short story is evident here in the tightness of scenes and incidents, but strung together they form a love story that is heavy with melodrama and very predictable."

D36   Keith, W.J. "Where Men and Mountains Meet." Rev. of SMT and JS. *Canadian Forum* June–July 1978: 27–28.

"Until now, O'Hagan has been the proverbial prophet without honour in his own country. . . . At long last, [he] seems to be coming into his own. . . . [JS contains] tales of the frontier — tough, often violent, but with a strong sense of human solidarity in the face of an inscrutable and frequently dangerous natural world. . . . *The School-Marm Tree* is a slighter achievement than *Tay John*, but, if read on its own terms, it will be recognized as a uniquely beautiful moral fable. Not the least of its merits is that it reveals O'Hagan as a little less enigmatic than the wilderness and mountains about which he writes."

D37   Weaver, Robert. Rev. of SMT and JS. *Canadian Reader* July 1978: 7–9.

"Howard O'Hagan is one of those writers who has been praised by the critics and ignored by the public. (I can think of two other Canadian novelists . . . who must have had similarly frustrating careers: Sinclair Ross . . . and Ernest Buckler . . .). Reading the stories in *The Woman Who Got On at Jasper Station* again after so many years was a pleasant experience. The stories are not dated, and O'Hagan's firm, clean prose hasn't faded." SMT is "both a very interesting and a curious work. It leaves the reader with a strong sense of ambiguity."

D38   Bilan, R.P. Rev. of SMT. *University of Toronto Quarterly* 47 (1978): 331–32.

"O'Hagan is a masterly story-teller and the narrative is continuously lively and interesting. There are some nice touches in O'Hagan's presentation of life in Yellowhead in 1925; in a scene in the beer parlour we see how all the characters and not just Selva are locked in their dreams. Further, O'Hagan succeeds in dealing frankly with his heroine's openly sexual nature. . . . [However,] there is an unduly schematic quality to the book, which becomes obvious in the characterization."

D39 Mills, John. Rev. of SMT and JS. *Fiddlehead* 20 (1978): 126–29.

"[T]he intensity of O'Hagan's style lifts these tales [in JS] above the level of a mere adventure story. His feeling for the wilderness, his descriptions of it, is always subordinated to the revelation of human behaviour and idiosyncrasy. . . . [SMT] lacks the tension of the stories, it is overwritten in places, and it is marred by a curious amateurishness. . . . It is, nevertheless, an interesting and entertaining work and ought to help its author to establish his reputation as one of the country's most distinguished writers."

D40 Rev. of SMT. *Canadian Author and Bookman* 54.1 (1978): 28–29.

"O'Hagan writes a fastidiously-wrought prose. He is particularly good at choosing apt, original metaphors. . . . The novel is a rich mine of gems. . . . I am enthusiastic about this novel; it is one of the best to cross my desk during several years of book reviewing. I predict it will become a Canadian classic."

D41 Harrison, Dick. "The O'Hagan Range." Rev. of SMT and JS. *Canadian Literature* 81 (1979): 116–18.

Harrison talks about "the considerable range of O'Hagan's stories," exemplified in the first and last stories in JS, "The Tepee" and "The Woman Who Got On at Jasper Station": "the two stories, in effect, take the reader a good distance from the world of *Tay John* toward that of *The School-Marm Tree*. . . . Like his contemporaries Sinclair Ross and Georges Bugnet, O'Hagan has worked without the stimulation of a lively critical response or the assurance of an intelligent readership among his countrymen. We should be grateful that *The School-Marm Tree* is a good novel; we should not hold it against O'Hagan that he once published a great novel like *Tay John*."

## Index to Critics Listed in the Bibliography

Mayhew, Anne  D9
Mills, John  D39
Minni, C.D.  D29
Mitchell, Ken  C29, C40
Monkman, Leslie  C14
Morash, Gordon  D21, D35
Morley, Patricia  C8
Moss, John  C15

Novak, Barbara  D32
Nowosad, Frank  C19

Oboler, Eli  D15
Ondaatje, Michael  C9, C35

Page, P.K.  C13
Peel, Bruce  D18
Powers, Gordon  D27

Roberts, Kevin  C41
Robertson, George  D10
Robinson, Jack  C30, C38

Schmuck, John  D8
Scobie, Stephen  C36
Skelton, Robin  C31
Smith, A.J.M.  C7
Stouck, David  C23, C32
Stow, Glenys  D13
Swinnerton, Frank  D2

Tanner, Ella  C1, C39
Thompson, John  D25

W., H.M.  D22
Watt, F.W.  D11
Weaver, Robert  D37
Wigod, Rebecca  C42
Woodcock, George  D12, D30

# LIST OF CONTRIBUTORS

RICHARD ARNOLD teaches English at Malaspina College, Nanaimo, British Columbia.

PETER JAMES CLARK has an MA in English from the University of Victoria, British Columbia; he is a doctoral student at the University of British Columbia.

LOVAT DICKSON was an author, editor, and publisher of distinction, holder of the Order of Canada, and Fellow of the Royal Society of Canada.

MARGERY FEE teaches English at Queen's University, Kingston, Ontario.

RONALD GRANOFSKY teaches English at McMaster University, Hamilton, Ontario.

W.J. KEITH is professor of English at University College, University of Toronto.

KEITH MAILLARD, the author of several novels, including *Two Strand River*, *Alex Driving South*, *The Knife in My Hands*, *Cutting Through*, and *Motet*, teaches in the Department of Creative Writing, University of British Columbia.

RALPH MAUD teaches English at Simon Fraser University, Burnaby, British Columbia.

CHRIS PETTER is the archivist at the Macpherson Library, University of Victoria, Victoria, British Columbia.

E.W. STRONG is emeritus professor, University of California, and former Mills Professor of Philosophy, University of California, Berkeley.